T0312308

Cambridge Elements ≡

Elements in the Philosophy of Immanuel Kant
edited by
Desmond Hogan
Princeton University
Howard Williams
University of Cardiff
Allen Wood
Indiana University

KANT'S LATE PHILOSOPHY OF NATURE

The Opus postumum

Stephen Howard
KU Leuven

CAMBRIDGE
UNIVERSITY PRESS

Shaftesbury Road, Cambridge CB2 8EA, United Kingdom

One Liberty Plaza, 20th Floor, New York, NY 10006, USA

477 Williamstown Road, Port Melbourne, VIC 3207, Australia

314–321, 3rd Floor, Plot 3, Splendor Forum, Jasola District Centre, New Delhi – 110025, India

103 Penang Road, #05–06/07, Visioncrest Commercial, Singapore 238467

Cambridge University Press is part of Cambridge University Press & Assessment, a department of the University of Cambridge.

We share the University's mission to contribute to society through the pursuit of education, learning and research at the highest international levels of excellence.

www.cambridge.org
Information on this title: www.cambridge.org/9781009013765

DOI: 10.1017/9781009031028

© Stephen Howard 2023

This publication is in copyright. Subject to statutory exception and to the provisions of relevant collective licensing agreements, no reproduction of any part may take place without the written permission of Cambridge University Press & Assessment.

First published 2023

A catalogue record for this publication is available from the British Library.

ISBN 978-1-009-01376-5 Paperback
ISSN 2397-9461 (online)
ISSN 2514-3824 (print)

Cambridge University Press & Assessment has no responsibility for the persistence or accuracy of URLs for external or third-party internet websites referred to in this publication and does not guarantee that any content on such websites is, or will remain, accurate or appropriate.

Kant's Late Philosophy of Nature

The *Opus postumum*

Elements in the Philosophy of Immanuel Kant

DOI: 10.1017/9781009031028
First published online: February 2023

Stephen Howard
KU Leuven
Author for correspondence: Stephen Howard, stephen.howard@kuleuven.be

Abstract: Kant's final drafts, known as his *Opus postumum,* attempt to make what he calls a "transition from the metaphysical foundations of natural science to physics." Interpreters broadly agree that in this project Kant seeks to connect the general a priori principles of natural science, as set out in the major critical works, to the specific results of empirical physics. Beyond this, however, basic interpretative issues remain controversial. This Element outlines a framework that aims to combine the systematic ambition of early twentieth-century readings with the rigor of more recent studies. The author argues that a question that has animated much recent scholarship – which 'gap' in Kant's previous philosophy does the Opus postumum seek to fill? – can be profitably set aside. In its place, renewed attention should be given to a crucial part of the manuscript, fascicles X/XI, and to the problematic 'arrival point' of the transition, namely, Kant's question: What is physics?

Keywords: Kant, *Opus postumum*, transition, metaphysical foundations, philosophy of nature

© Stephen Howard 2023

ISBNs: 9781009013765 (PB), 9781009031028 (OC)
ISSNs: 2397-9461 (online), 2514-3824 (print)

Contents

1 Introduction   1

2 A Sketch of the Reception History   5

3 'Gap' or Transition Problem?   10

4 The Form of the Transition Problem   23

5 What Is Physics?   27

6 Conclusion   52

Appendix: How to Read the *Opus postumum*   56

References   64

1 Introduction

What we call Kant's *Opus postumum* is, in the simplest terms, a pile of 527 handwritten pages of drafts toward a work that the philosopher did not live to complete. Kant chiefly worked on the project between 1796 and 1801, although the earliest related pages date to 1786, the year in which he published the *Metaphysical Foundations of Natural Science*, and the latest to 1803, the year before his death. He grouped the pages into twelve fascicles (in German, *Konvolute*), enclosed in folded sheets, on two of which he wrote further notes. The fascicle wrappers are numbered in another hand. This will have occurred at some point during the famously circuitous journey of the manuscript as it passed from Kant's descendants via Königsberg librarian Rudolf Reicke to Pastor Albrecht Krause, whose family owned it when it was published in the Academy edition of Kant's works in 1936–8.[1] During this journey, many pages were apparently shuffled within and between the fascicles. Artur Buchenau and Gerhard Lehmann, who edited the 1936–8 Academy edition (after Erich Adickes resigned due to editorial disagreements), took the questionable decision to publish Kant's manuscript in the order that they found the pages in the fascicles. The combination of the dense and repetitive character of Kant's drafts with the nonchronological ordering of the existing Academy edition makes the *Opus postumum* a challenging text to read, to say the least.

Given the state of the text, it is no surprise that there are heated debates over many basic questions of interpretation. Perhaps the most fundamental questions are methodological. Should the drafts be treated as a 'work,' or as a disconnected series of sketches, or as something in between? If a work or an effort toward one, is it 'critical' or 'postcritical': does it primarily adhere to, modify, or even abandon the major doctrines of the three *Critiques*? Should the *Opus postumum* be taken seriously at all, or, following a view notoriously expressed by Kuno Fischer, should it be dismissed as a product of the older Kant's senility? Basic questions about the content of the drafts are just as controversial: what is the problem, or what are the problems, with which Kant is concerned?

A key issue facing any interpretation of the *Opus postumum* is whether it takes the drafts to contain a unified project. Is Kant consistently attempting to resolve a single problem? If so, which? The subject matter of the drafts ranges from the classification of physical properties and types of forces, to attempts to prove the existence of a universally distributed 'ether,' to the so-called

---

[1] The story is told by Adickes (1920: 1–35), Stark (1993: 54–9, 100–29), Förster (in Kant [1993]: xvi–xxiii), and Basile (2013: 459–98). The manuscript reached its current home in the Berlin Staatsbibliothek in 1999.

Selbstsetzungslehre, according to which the thinking subject posits itself in space and time, to innumerable definitions of 'physics' and 'transcendental philosophy,' to a system of the ideas of God, world, and man-in-the-world. And this list of themes barely scratches the surface: we also find reflections on organisms, machines, the matter of light, teleology, freedom, Spinoza, the Persian prophet Zoroaster, the rights or duties of God, the categorical imperative, and innumerable other subjects. How can we reconcile any single aim that might unify the project with the great diversity of topics, dilemmas, and solutions that Kant explores?

This Element proposes some answers to these large questions. Very little is uncontroversial in *Opus postumum* scholarship, but one minimal point on which interpreters agree is that Kant seeks to connect the general a priori foundations of natural science, which he outlined in the three *Critiques* and the *Metaphysical Foundations of Natural Science*, with the specific results of empirical physics. Kant calls this the problem of the 'transition' (*Übergang*). His standard formulation for his task in the late project is the "transition from the metaphysical foundations of natural science to physics." The present Element aims to explain this formulation. I make my case in two steps. First, Sections 2, 3, and 4 address central methodological issues facing the reader of the drafts. Second, the long Section 5 examines the philosophical developments in what I claim is a crucial phase of Kant's struggle with the transition problem.

Throughout, and particularly in the first step, I make extensive reference to the history of *Opus postumum* scholarship. I do so because the unfinished and messy state of Kant's drafts exacerbates a feature of all historical philosophical texts: we cannot read them in isolation from the interpretations and debates that have sedimented around them over the centuries. I give particular attention to the German-language literature, which contains insights and debates that are sometimes unjustly overlooked by Anglophone scholars. The existing scholarship is invaluable for making sense of the chaotic text. But it has also imposed certain interpretative tendencies that need to be identified, and in some cases loosened, if we want to gain a more faithful understanding of Kant's drafts.

Accordingly, Section 2 critically surveys the history of *Opus postumum* scholarship since the beginning of the twentieth century. My survey identifies a break in the literature around 1970. Earlier scholars had systematizing ambitions: they made grand claims about the governing concern of Kant's late project, incorporating all the phases of the drafts into their argument. In doing so, however, they tended to impose their own philosophical interests onto the drafts. After 1970, following the work of Burkhard Tuschling, interpreters became more attentive to the historical development of the drafts and generally restricted their claims to particular problems and phases in Kant's project.

I argue that it is worth attempting to rehabilitate the systematizing ambitions of the early twentieth-century scholarship, while maintaining the historical and textual sensitivity of more recent work.

Section 3 engages further with the existing literature by challenging an assumption common to recent interpretations. Over the last fifty years, it has become standard to read the *Opus postumum* as Kant's effort to solve problems left over from his earlier works. This interpretative orthodoxy revolves around the question of the 'gap' in Kant's previous philosophy that the late project is said to attempt to fill. After examining Kant's notions of 'gap' and 'transition,' I argue that the recent debate arises from an ambiguity in the term 'gap' (*Lücke*). The term can denote either a failing or, more neutrally, a separation. On my reading, it is this second, neutral sense of 'gap' that is at stake in the drafts. Kant's new transition-science aims to bridge the separation between the distinct domains of the metaphysical foundations of natural science and physics. This means, I contend, that the 'gap problem' as it is usually understood can be profitably set aside, allowing us to focus more closely on the immanent development of Kant's transition project.

Section 4 goes on to make a more general methodological proposal: that we should distinguish between the stable form of the transition project and its shifting content. The form of the project is expressed in Kant's consistent formulation of his problem: the "transition from the metaphysical foundations of natural science to physics." However, all three elements of this formulation – the metaphysical foundations, physics, and the transition between them – are repeatedly rethought. The meanings of these terms shift under the pressure of the difficulties that Kant faces, and as a result of his efforts to address these difficulties in the project. My proposed approach to the transition problem aims to do justice both to the dynamic, exploratory character of Kant's drafts and to his intention to produce a 'work' that would solve the various problems at stake in the transition to physics.

The second main step of my discussion, Section 5, turns to what I claim is a key moment in Kant's attempts to solve the transition problem. In light of the previous section's depiction of the form of the problem, I suggest that we should tackle the relatively neglected question of the *arrival point* of the transition, namely, physics. I thus advocate a renewed focus on a specific phase of the drafts, fascicles X/XI of August 1799 to April 1800, in which Kant reflects intensely on the meaning of physics.[2] Commentators have typically

---

[2] I divide the *Opus postumum* into five chronological periods: 'Preparatory work and *Oktaventwurf*' (1786–96), 'Elementary system' (July 1797–May 1799), 'Ether proofs' (May 1799–August 1799), 'Fascicles X/XI' (August 1799–April 1800), and 'Fascicles VII/I' (April 1800–February 1803). For more on these phases and their dates, see Appendix, section A.2.

assumed that 'physics' in the *Opus postumum* can be understood in an everyday sense: as an empirical science that observes and experiments upon physical phenomena. That may be the case in the early phases of the drafts. However, in fascicles X/XI, Kant explores conceiving of physics in unfamiliar and much broader new ways. He distinguishes between various types of systems of physics, and he stretches the notion of physics in the directions of psychology and cosmology, such that it newly encompasses the forces of the perceiving subject and the idea of the totality of appearances. By rethinking physics in this way, I argue, Kant attempts to resolve the transition problem by determining how empirical physics can itself be systematic. He makes various attempts to distinguish the fixed, a priori elements of physics from its ever-increasing and unforeseeable empirical results.

It may be helpful to indicate, in a preliminary manner, what I consider to be the philosophical stakes of this phase of Kant's late project. As mentioned, I shall argue that the *Opus postumum* is best read not as an attempt to resolve problems left over from the critical works, but as a substantially new endeavor. But this does not mean, of course, that the drafts are independent of the critical philosophy. Which aspects of Kant's earlier thought, then, are most relevant to these late reflections on physics? One interpretative option would be to turn to the debate in the current literature over whether, and how, Kant justifies the necessity of particular, empirical laws of nature, as distinct from general transcendental laws.[3] However, although I believe that further consideration of the *Opus postumum* and its transition problem could enrich this debate, I do not think that the debate provides the most helpful lens through which to see what is at stake in Kant's late project. Kant is not expressly concerned with whether particular laws of nature can be known as necessary or merely as Humean regularities. In my view, it is more illuminating to understand Kant to be grappling in the *Opus postumum* with the implications and difficulties of his own conception of science.

According to Kant, all sciences are inherently *systematic*. The first *Critique* asserts that "systematic unity is that which first makes everyday cognition into science" (A832/B860).[4] A system is "the unity of manifold cognitions under an idea." Such an idea is the "rational concept of the form of a whole" that should determine a priori "the extent [*Umfang*] of the manifold as well as the places of the

---

[3] Briefly put, three sources of the necessity of (certain) particular laws have been argued for: the best system of all laws (defended by Buchdahl and Kitcher), derivation from the categories (Friedman), or the essences or natures of things (Watkins and Kreines). For an overview of this debate, see Messina 2017. Recent interventions include McNulty 2015, Breitenbach 2018, and Engelhard 2018.

[4] For the referencing conventions used in this Element, see the References section.

parts with respect to each other" (A832/B860, cf. A645/B673).[5] On the interpretation that I shall defend, the *Opus postumum* contains Kant's own, generally overlooked, attempts to address the question of how empirical physics can be systematic. Kant's criterion of systematicity evidently requires some aspects of empirical physics to be known in advance of experience. But, in practice, what does it mean for the manifold and interrelation of the objects of physics to be determined a priori? In the terms that Kant often uses, as we shall see, this is the question of how far the results of empirical physics can be *anticipated* prior to experience, and whether such anticipation is material or merely formal.

As almost every commentator on the *Opus postumum* has pointed out, Kant does not first address this issue in this text. It is treated in different ways in the *Metaphysical Foundations* and the *Critique of Judgment*. However, the transition project differs from the main body of the *Metaphysical Foundations* in that Kant is no longer concerned with matter in general but with the *specific properties* of matter (see Sections 4.2 and 5.4 below). And it differs from the third *Critique* in that Kant's focus is not the systematicity of nature for the sake of reflecting judgment, but the systematicity of *physics*. This, as we shall see, requires 'bridging' concepts other than the principle of purposiveness.[6]

Following the extended discussion of Kant's exploration of physics in Section 5, I return in the conclusion (Section 6) to a broader question. The problem at stake in the *Opus postumum*, on my account, may seem similar to the problem that early logical positivists sought to solve with the notion of the 'constitutive' or 'relativized' a priori. In both cases, at issue is how to reconcile the unforeseeable developments of an empirical science with a certain conception of a priori conditions. I will claim, however, that Kant's solution to the problem contrasts instructively with that of his later followers and critics.

Although this Element situates itself throughout in the history of existing interpretations, the best way to engage with Kant's final project is, of course, simply to read it. To help with this, the book ends with an Appendix, "How to read the *Opus postumum*."

2 A Sketch of the Reception History

This section provides an overview of the broad tendencies in the history of scholarship on the *Opus postumum*. In my view, a fundamental methodological break takes place around 1970. By returning to the early twentieth-century

---

[5] For discussion of Kant's conception of systematicity prior to the *Opus postumum*, see Zöller 2001 and Sturm 2009: 131–82.

[6] This is, of course, a quick treatment of questions that have been heavily debated in the literature. I agree with Förster (2000: 5–11) and Emundts (2004: 59–66) when they insist on significant differences between the aims of the *Opus postumum* and the *Critique of Judgment*.

interpretations, I intend to propose which aspects of these readings are worth rehabilitating and which should be avoided. This will set the scene for my discussion, in Section 3, of the 'gap problem,' which has been central to debates in the literature since 1970.

The major early twentieth-century interpretations had clear systematizing intentions. This is evident in the first significant study of the *Opus postumum*, Adickes' 855-page book, published a decade and a half before the Academy edition (Adickes 1920). Adickes splits Kant's project into a "predominantly natural-scientific and natural-philosophical part" and a "metaphysical–epistemological part." In line with his later conclusions in *Kant als Naturforscher* (1924–5), Adickes portrays Kant as a feeble natural philosopher but an insightful metaphysician. The metaphysical innovations developed in the *Opus postumum* are, according to Adickes (1920: 849, 239), Kant's realist account of things in themselves, presented "for once completely consistently, from a strict transcendental-philosophical (epistemological) standpoint," and his doctrine of "double affection," according to which the I or self is affected both "through things in themselves and through appearances."

Adickes is here responding to the earlier interpretation of Hans Vaihinger, who claimed that the problem of double affection was an aporia running through Kant's philosophy. Vaihinger contends that only in the final fascicles of the *Opus postumum* does Kant adequately address the problem of double affection. He is said to do so by conceiving of things in themselves as "fictions," which, conveniently enough, coheres with Vaihinger's own philosophy of the 'as if' (Vaihinger 1911: 721–33, see Basile 2013: 34–41). Adickes follows Vaihinger in viewing the problem of double affection as "the key to Kant's epistemology" (see Adickes 1929). But he has an opposed interpretation of Kant's solution: he claims that Kant has a realist rather than a fictionalist conception of things in themselves. Adickes develops this point in his interpretation of the *Opus postumum* and, particularly, with regard to what he calls the "new deduction" in fascicles X/XI (August 1799–April 1800).[7] He dedicates over 100 pages to the topic, although he ultimately considers Kant's efforts to result in failure (Adickes 1920: 235–362). This new deduction, Adickes claims, is where Kant attempts to show how the empirical self is affected by complexes of forces, in a way that is distinct from how things in themselves affect the self in itself.[8] The subject's *self*-affection is central to this new deduction (Adickes 1920: 248–79). In Adickes' view, Kant's more successful theory of self-affection then appears in the final fascicles VII/I.

---

[7] On my divisions of the phases of the drafts, see footnote 2 and Appendix, section A.2.

[8] Adickes 1920: 237–40; for discussions, see Stang 2013: 792–8 and Basile 2019: 3641–5.

The details of this debate over so-called double affection, which rarely interests scholars today, need not detain us further.[9] Relevant for our purposes is how Vaihinger and Adickes divide up Kant's late drafts in order to justify their conceptions of the philosophical project therein. Adickes' distinction between the natural-scientific and metaphysical halves of Kant's manuscript is a modification of Vaihinger's more radical reading. Vaihinger (1891: 734) claims that the *Opus postumum* contains two entirely separate works: a "special natural-philosophical" work and a "general transcendental-philosophical" one.[10] Everything prior to April 1800 is said to belong to the first work; the writings after this date, namely, fascicles VII/I, belong to the second. In Vaihinger's eyes, only the second work is philosophically significant. Although his chronological division suggests that fascicles X/XI are part of the first 'work,' Vaihinger's discussion of double affection almost exclusively cites these fascicles, suggesting they should be placed in the second 'work' (see Basile 2019: 3639 n.5). Despite their disagreements, then, both Vaihinger and Adickes see fascicles X/XI as the pivotal moment in Kant's final project; and both consider the ideas developed there to culminate in the 'properly philosophical' fascicles VII/I.

The question of the so-called new deduction in fascicles X/XI is crucial for two further early systematizing interpretations, those of Herman J. de Vleeschauwer and Gerhard Lehmann. De Vleeschauwer (1937: 569) considers fascicles X/XI to pursue a transcendental deduction of "the forces and elementary properties of matter." This is at the heart of "the third edition of the *Critique of Pure Reason*" that he contends can be found in the *Opus postumum*, particularly the new theory of experience that appears in Kant's doctrine of self-positing (*Selbstsetzungslehre*) (de Vleeschauwer 1937: 565, 579–80). While deeply influenced by Adickes' interpretation, de Vleeschauwer shifts the so-called new deduction away from Adickes' concern with double affection and the realist interpretation of things in themselves to instead stress what he sees as Kant's new proximity to Fichte.

Lehmann's interpretation has more distance from the questions posed by Vaihinger and Adickes, but he too continues to call fascicles X/XI a "new deduction," indeed, a deduction of the categories (Lehmann 1969: 317).[11] Lehmann (1969: 278–84) calls the new deduction the "fundamental philosophical

---

[9] For further discussion of this topic in the *Opus postumum*, however, see Hall 2015: 154–206 and Basile 2019. Stang (2015) seeks to revive the issue more systematically; he explicitly avoids referring to Kant's late drafts.

[10] On this point Vaihinger follows Krause, whose book he is here reviewing.

[11] When citing Lehmann in this Element I refer to the 1969 collection of his essays. Those I cite are: "Ganzheitsbegriff und Weltidee in Kants *Opus postumum*" (1936; Lehmann 1969: 247–71), "Das philosophische Grundproblem in Kants Nachlaßwerk" (1937; Lehmann 1969: 272–88), "Kants Nachlaßwerk und die *Kritik der Urteilskraft*" (1939; Lehmann 1969: 295–373), and "Zur Frage der Spätentwicklung Kants" (1963; Lehmann 1969: 393–408).

problem" of the *Opus postumum*. Admitting that it is less easy to succinctly sum up than the "old deduction," Lehmann characterizes the central point of the new deduction in various ways.[12] Many of the topics that Lehmann highlights do indeed seem to be novel concerns for Kant; we shall return to them in Section 5. But at no point does Lehmann justify understanding the alleged new deduction as a deduction: the relationship to the "old deduction," and what is deduced and how, remains obscure. Neither does Lehmann clarify how his conception of the new deduction relates to a central theme of his interpretation, the relationship between the *Opus postumum* and the third *Critique*.[13]

There is evidently a motley series of doctrines contained under the title of the 'new deduction' in these early interpretations. As Hansgeorg Hoppe (1969: 114) and Vittorio Mathieu (1989: 137) later rightly state, the drafts in question bear little resemblance to any kind of a deduction. The indeterminate notion of a 'new deduction' appears to function as a means for Adickes, de Vleeschauwer, and Lehmann to impose their own interests onto the drafts. Nevertheless, despite their limitations, these early interpretations are notable for two reasons: they attempt *systematizing interpretations* of the overall project of Kant's late drafts and they place *fascicles X/XI* at the centre of their readings.

Both of these tendencies dwindle in the scholarship from 1970 onwards. An important stimulus for the new approach is the work of Burkhard Tuschling. According to Tuschling (1971: 11–12), a systematically oriented interpretation is "impossible." He offers three reasons for this. First, we should not conflate passages from different phases without considering whether Kant might not be giving different meanings to the same phrases. Tuschling's example, key to his book, is that in the late drafts the clause "metaphysical foundations of natural science" does not refer to Kant's 1786 work. Second, we should avoid discussing the drafts in an order determined by external principles; he notes that Lehmann criticizes Adickes for this in the introduction to the Academy edition (22:771–2). Third, we should not interpret certain phases of the drafts without considering the phases that precede them, in the way that Adickes, de Vleeschauwer, and Lehmann treat the final fascicles X/XI, VII, and I. Tuschling (1971: 13) advocates instead a "historical" interpretation. By this he means, on the one hand, describing the development of Kant's train of

---

[12] Namely, that it should justify: the principle of the unity of experience; the claim that perceptions belong to the system of moving forces and vice versa; the concepts of the appearance of the appearance, sensible space, the material anticipation of experience, and the act-correspondence of the object; the objectification of the concrete self-constitution of the subject; the reaction theory of perceptions and moving forces and the identification of two steps of appearance (Lehmann 1969: 258, 259, 280, 283–4, 365).

[13] Lehmann (1969: 405) does draw a connection between the concepts of organism, system, and totality, but in my view the issue remains underdetermined.

thought in all its complexity, and, on the other, contextualizing this description in relation to Kant's earlier writings and those of his contemporaries.

No one would deny that we should avoid the errors that Tuschling identifies, or that his "historical" approach can usefully guard against them. However, it is less clear that the problems he diagnoses afflict all possible systematizing interpretations and render them futile. Nor is it obvious that a historical sensitivity to the internal development of the drafts and to their context is incompatible with the attempt to read the *Opus postumum* systematically. Nevertheless, subsequent studies have tended to follow Tuschling in eschewing overarching accounts of the project of the drafts. Eckart Förster's book, still the most important English-language work on Kant's late drafts, takes its methodological lead from Heinz Heimsoeth, who recommended that scholars produce a series of focused investigations into delimited issues in the *Opus postumum* (Förster 2000: x; see also Edwards 1991: 96 n.9). This is indeed the approach of the major studies published since 1970, all of which treat only particular problems in specific phases of the drafts.[14]

The restricted scope of the studies of the past fifty years is evident in their textual basis. Tuschling (1971) and Dina Emundts (2004) address only the drafts prior to August 1799; that is, their books do not reach fascicles X/XI. Jeffrey Edwards (2000, see also 2004: 162 n.14) skips fascicles X/XI to focus on the ether proofs and fascicle I either side of them. Although Förster (2000) endeavors to cover all the phases of the drafts, he considers Kant's innovations to be found in two phases: the ether proofs of May to August 1799 and the *Selbstsetzungslehre*, which is usually located in fascicle VII of April to December 1800. Förster (2000: 101–16, particularly 106–7) discusses fascicles X/XI only insofar as they shed light on the *Selbstsetzungslehre*. He thus disregards the specific investigations that Kant pursues in fascicles X/XI.

The scholarship that has appeared in the wake of Tuschling's work is more rigorous and careful than the early twentieth-century interpretations, but it also lacks the earlier scholarship's systematizing ambitions; it is less willing to try to encompass all phases of the drafts and determine the overarching problem with which Kant is grappling.[15] The present Element is motivated by a sense that the time is ripe to attempt this once more. Such a synoptic interpretation would

---

[14] Tuschling 1971, Friedman 1992, Emundts 2004, Edwards 2008, Hall 2014, and Thorndike 2018.

[15] There are three notable exceptions to my survey of the tendencies in twentieth-century *Opus postumum* scholarship. First, Vittorio Mathieu, who, in his Italian-language study of 1958 and a revised and condensed German version in 1989, goes further than other scholars of the postwar period in the direction of a systematizing interpretation of the *Opus postumum*. He stands at the crossroads of the 'old' and 'new' approaches in the scholarship, combining close reading of passages and a sensitivity to the developmental character of the drafts with claims about Kant's overall intentions. I will regularly return to his book in what follows, including his methodological proposals (Appendix, section A.1). However, his attempt to speculatively reconstruct Kant's final 'work' seems to me over-ambitious (Mathieu 1989: 79–83; see Section 5.9). Second,

rehabilitate something of the ambition of early scholarship, as well as its textual basis, by placing fascicles X/XI back at the heart of Kant's transition project. Like the early twentieth-century readers of the *Opus postumum*, I consider fascicles X/XI to contain Kant's most intriguing and productive reflections: perhaps the final concerted intellectual effort of a great philosopher. However, any rehabilitation of a systematizing approach must take into account the results of the scholarship since 1970 and emulate its rigorous attention to the historical development of Kant's text. We should avoid the tendency of early interpreters to appropriate the drafts for their own philosophical interests, whether double affection, Fichtean idealism, or organized nature. I aim here to avoid imposing external concerns onto Kant's final project. Instead, we shall follow as closely as possible the train of thought in the drafts: the repetitions, variations, and transformations of Kant's claims as he grapples with the problem, which the next section will examine more closely, of the 'transition.'

It is not a coincidence that the scholarship since 1970, which takes a more piecemeal approach to the drafts and pays little attention to fascicles X/XI, is primarily concerned with the question of the 'gap': the failing in his previous philosophy that Kant is said to rectify in the *Opus postumum*. This is because the problem of the gap, to which we turn next, provides an alternative way to make sense of the drafts, in place of the systematizing claims of earlier interpreters. That is, one can provide a coherent interpretation, despite attending only to particular periods and delimited issues in the drafts, *if* one assumes that Kant is primarily concerned with rectifying a problem in his earlier works. The question of the gap and its filling has thus become an anchoring point for recent interpretations. The next section will advocate abandoning this methodological orthodoxy of recent *Opus postumum* scholarship.

3 'Gap' or Transition Problem?

3.1 The Question of the Gap

Scholarship on the *Opus postumum* in the last fifty years has been particularly stimulated by Kant's comments about his final project in two letters of 1798. To Christian Garve on September 21, 1798, Kant writes that the task he is working

---

Hansgeorg Hoppe (1969, 1991), who focuses on fascicles X/XI to interpret the *Opus postumum* as a theory of physics. I critically discuss Hoppe's interpretation in Section 5.8, including a debate between Hoppe and Mathieu. Finally, Karin Gloy (1976), who seeks to systematically reconstruct Kant's philosophy of nature according to its sources, extent, and limits on the basis of the first *Critique*, the *Metaphysical Foundations*, and the *Opus postumum*. Insofar as it is concerned with the *Opus postumum*, Gloy's study, which does not refer to Tuschling's book, shares with the early twentieth-century scholarship both a systematizing orientation and a lack of attention to the developmental character of the drafts.

on concerns the transition from the metaphysical foundations of natural science to physics. He states that this task "must be resolved, because otherwise there would be a gap (*Lücke*) in the system of transcendental philosophy."[16] He also admits, in a much-cited phrase, to feeling a "pain like that of Tantalus, which is however not without hope," when he sees before him the "not-yet fully settled account, which concerns the whole of philosophy (with regard to both end and means)" (12:257). The transition project is here linked to a gap, something lacking, in the system of transcendental philosophy, and seems to be equated with Kant's unpaid bill regarding the whole of philosophy.

A month later, Kant makes similar points in a letter to Johann Kiesewetter. He writes that, although old and worn out by his official duties, he feels he has sufficient powers to complete his transition project, which will "conclude his critical business and fill a gap that still remains." This entails elaborating the transition "as a proper part of *philosophia naturalis*, which the system should not lack [*der im System nicht mangeln darf*]" (12:258). As in the letter to Garve, Kant refers to the need to fill a gap and indicates that something is missing in the system of philosophy. In the letter to Kiesewetter, the gap and the transition project are newly linked to the "critical business." These are exactly the words Kant used at the end of the Preface to the *Critique of Judgment*, when he announced that the third *Critique* completes his "whole critical business," enabling him to "proceed [*schreiten*] without delay to the doctrinal [part]" (5:170). Between 1790 and 1798, then, Kant appears to have changed his mind as to whether the critical philosophy has been concluded. His work on the transition project and the gap at stake seems to have spurred a return to the critical philosophy, implying that the unpaid bill he mentions to Garve concerns a problem in his own earlier work.

This is the standard interpretation of the 1798 letters, which we shall shortly reexamine (Section 3.4). A significant amount of the scholarship since 1970 takes this interpretation of the letters as its point of departure and seeks to identify the 'gap' in Kant's previous philosophy that the transition project aims to fill. This line of research was arguably initiated by Tuschling, who argues that the *Opus postumum* drafts attempt a "radical correction" of the matter theory of the *Metaphysical Foundations*. For Tuschling, the drafts are a self-critique resulting from Kant's identification of an inescapable "circle" in his account of how density differs in different matters, an issue highlighted by critical initial reviews of the *Metaphysical Foundations*.[17] Tuschling refers regularly but

---

[16] I consistently translate *Lücke* as 'gap' and *Kluft* as 'gulf.'

[17] Tuschling 1971: 46; see 11:376. The circularity in Kant's 1786 theory of density emerges, as Förster (2000: 33) puts it, in that "the intensity of the attractive force [of a piece of matter] must

without great emphasis to the "gap" in the system of the critical philosophy, implying that Kant's self-critique aimed to rectify this.[18]

It is in Förster's work that the problem of the gap is first explicitly made the starting point of an interpretation. For Förster (1987, 2000: 61, 70–2), the gap appears when Kant recognizes the circularity problem and sees a new need to supplement the Schematism chapter to prove the objective reality of objects of outer sense. In subsequent scholarship, the character of the gap becomes a topic of intense debate. Michael Friedman (1992: 256–63, 2003: 221–5) locates it between the constitutive and regulative approaches of the *Metaphysical Foundations* and the third *Critique*. Critical responses to Friedman's account are offered by Kenneth Westphal (1995), Förster (2000: 188–90, 2003: 234–5), and Edwards (2004: 178–85). Like Friedman, Frederick Beiser (2002: 182–5) locates the gap between the understanding's general a priori laws and the specific empirical laws of nature, and in the inadequacy of the third *Critique*'s regulative principle of reflective judgment. Bryan Wesley Hall (2014: 50–3) considers the gap to be between Kant's two concepts of substance. Emundts (2004: 15, 21–31, 58), although she does not take the 1798 letters as her starting point, locates the gap in Kant's need to replace the General Remark of the Dynamics chapter of the *Metaphysical Foundations* in order to explain the specific varieties of matter and systematically incorporate them into his theory of matter.[19] Oliver Thorndike (2018: 53–4, 106–8) has a similar account to Emundts with regard to Kant's transition project in theoretical philosophy.

The debate over the location and nature of the gap has undoubtedly provided valuable insights into the relations between Kant's late drafts and his earlier views. Nevertheless, I shall advocate setting aside the gap problem to allow a closer focus on the problem of the *transition* and the conceptual resources with which Kant attempts to solve it. We can first examine Kant's concept of 'transition,' before and in the *Opus postumum* drafts, before using this to reevaluate the question of the gap. I shall argue that the debate over the gap problem rests on an ambiguity in the term *Lücke*, and that the gap at stake in the transition project is not best understood as a failing in Kant's earlier philosophy.

3.2 'Transition' in Kant's Writings of 1781–1796

The term 'transition' (*Übergang*) features regularly in the major published works. I suggest that we can distinguish four main contexts in which it is used. First, 'transition' often features in a section title. The term here simply

---

depend on [its] density, and density must in turn be the effect of attraction." For further discussion, see Tuschling 1971: 39–65, Förster 2000: 33–45, and Emundts 2004: 76–117.

[18] See Tuschling 1971: 8, 34, 180, 182, 189, and, most explicitly, 158–60.

[19] I return to Emundt's interpretation in Section 4.2.

signifies a movement between different parts of Kant's discussion; these parts are often aligned with different bodies of knowledge or different philosophical approaches. Notable examples are the titles of the three sections of the *Groundwork*.[20] A second way that Kant uses the term relates to different states of appearances, including their reality and negation.[21] Here, Kant is concerned with the continuity of experience through the transitions in states of either appearances or our cognitive states.

The transition between states of appearances relates to a third context in which Kant uses the term: his references to the principle of continuity. The principle entails that transitions between species, for example, do not occur through a leap but progress through all intermediate subspecies (*Zwischenarten*) (A658–60/B686–8). At the end of the chapter on the Postulates, Kant writes that the principle of continuity leads to two of the four principles that he inherits from traditional metaphysical cosmology: the principles that there is no leap and no gap in the series of appearances ("*in mundo non datur saltus . . . non datur hiatus*") (A228–9/B281). As Eric Watkins (2019: 207–8) has emphasized, Kant here claims that these cosmological principles hold for *experience*. Kant thus appropriates the cosmological principles of continuity to emphasize that there is always a smooth transition, that is, no gap and no leap, between appearances.

The fourth context in which Kant refers to 'transition' has greater systematic significance for the critical philosophy. At the beginning of the Transcendental Dialectic, Kant suggests that "perhaps the ideas make possible a transition from concepts of nature to the practical" (A329/B386). At this point in the first *Critique*, Kant sets aside the question of how the ideas of reason, particularly the transcendental ideas pertaining to the soul, world-whole, and God, can link the theoretical and moral interests of reason. He then returns in the Preface to the second *Critique* to the "transition to a completely different use" of reason, the transition between the speculative and practical use of reason (5:7). The concept of freedom, whose objective reality is revealed in the practical domain, is the "keystone" that makes this transition possible (5:3). Kant insists that his account does not intend "to fill in a gap in the critical system of speculative reason," but rather should show how the concept of freedom makes the coherence of the system evident (5:7).

Famously, the published introduction to the third *Critique* affirms that there is an "incalculable gulf" between the domains of nature and freedom (5:175). Kant claims that "no transition is possible" from the domain of nature to the domain

---

[20] "Transition from common rational to philosophical moral cognition"; "Transition from popular moral philosophy to metaphysics of morals"; "Transition from metaphysics of morals to the critique of pure practical reason" (4:393, 406, 446). Other examples are at A94/B124, B428, 5:244, 6:305.

[21] A100, A143/B182–3, A171/B212, A188/B231, A206–10/B251–5.

of freedom, but the inverse transition from freedom to nature *can* be made (5:176). The ground of possibility of this latter transition is reflective judgment and its principle of purposiveness. In both the second and third *Critiques*, Kant presents the domains of nature and freedom as the "sensible" and "supersensible" realms, respectively (5:5, 175–6, 196). The term 'supersensible' first appears in Kant's published writings in the "Orientation" essay of 1786 (see Schwaiger 2004: 338).

It is therefore with regard to various domains that Kant employs the concept of transition in the critical works: bodies of knowledge or subdisciplines of philosophy; cognitive states and appearances; different species; and the domains of the concepts of nature and freedom, otherwise called the sensible and the supersensible. The principle of continuity underpins all these transitions, because a transition should not be a leap (*Sprung*) (see A659/B687, A783/B811). It is instead an orderly movement between two different domains – which nevertheless remain separate.

Kant's writings from the mid-1790s on the transition to the supersensible have an instructive formal connection to the analyses of the transition to physics that appear shortly afterwards in the *Opus postumum* drafts, although as far as I am aware this connection has not been made in the literature to date.[22] In "What Real Progress?" (1793–5), the drafts of a response to the Berlin Academy's 1790 prize essay question on the progress of metaphysics, Kant defines metaphysics as "the science of progressing [*fortzuschreiten*], through reason, from cognition of the sensible to that of the supersensible" (20:260). In these drafts, playing on the Academy's question, Kant uses "progress" (*Fortschritt*) and "overstep" (*Überschritt*) in place of the "transition" referred to in the Introduction to the *Critique of Judgment*.[23] In both cases, however, the transition between the domains of nature and freedom is at stake. Employing an image from his discussions of the principle of continuity, Kant writes in the prize essay drafts that such a transit between these domains should not be a "dangerous leap" (20:272–3).

---

[22] In the course of arguing that a key context for the *Opus postumum* is the third *Critique*, Lehmann connects the late drafts to the transition from the sensible to the supersensible in Kant's 1790 work. Lehmann does not, however, mention the 1793–6 writings I shall discuss here (although he gives a page reference from "What Real Progress?" without naming these drafts: Lehmann 1969: 192). Basile (2013: 376–8) proposes that Kant became aware of the need for the *Opus postumum*'s "counterpart" to the transition from the sensible to the supersensible when he read Maimon's *Baco and Kant* (1790). As I lack the space to evaluate this interesting suggestion, I just note that Basile only refers to the third *Critique* with regard to the sensible–supersensible transition.

[23] Here and in what follows I translate *Überschritt* and *überschreiten* as 'overstep' and 'step over.' The terms can be translated more smoothly with 'transit,' 'pass,' or 'cross,' but the more literal renderings highlight Kant's regular play on 'step' (*Schritt, schreiten*) in the *Opus postumum*, as well as the sense of transgression, which I discuss in Section 3.3.

However, because we also cannot make "a continuous progress in the same order of principles" between these heterogenous domains, it is necessary to maintain "a progress-inhibiting cautious attention [*Fortschritt hemmende Bedenklichkeit*] at the boundaries of both domains" (20:273). These unfinished drafts do not reach a definite conclusion, but Kant often adheres to his previous view that only in practical philosophy is a transition to the supersensible possible (e.g. 20:277, 292, 301).

A year after setting aside the progress essay drafts, Kant published a polemical essay, "On A Superior Tone" (1796), criticizing Johann Georg Schlosser and his group of mystical Platonists. In the writings of these figures, Kant identifies "a certain mystical cadence, an overleap [*Übersprung*] (*salto mortale*) from concepts to the unthinkable" (8:398). The opening of the text makes clear that this "unthinkable" domain is, in Kant's usual terminology, that of the supersensible. He adds his now-standard claim that cognition of the supersensible, which is a "true mystery" from a theoretical perspective, is possible from a practical perspective.[24] The mystical Platonists, by contrast, lay claim to direct, speculative knowledge of the supersensible through intellectual intuition. They thus attempt a *salto mortale* or dangerous leap (8:389). This is the image used by Jacobi in the *Letters Concerning the Doctrine of Spinoza* (1785) to affirm a leap, beyond the conception of reason held by philosophers like Kant, to faith (see Schick 2006).

As we have seen, Kant denies in the first *Critique* that a leap (*salto*) is possible in the order of appearances when he appropriates the cosmological principle *in mundo non datur saltus*. The writings of the 1790s extend the principle of continuity to the question of the transition between theoretical cognition of the sensible and practical cognition of the supersensible. Such a transition between distinct domains should not be a dangerous leap but a careful passage according to principles. Such principles include the purposiveness examined in the third *Critique* and, more generally, those with which the critical philosophy determines the boundary of theoretical cognition.[25]

3.3 'Transition' in the *Opus postumum*

It is striking that Kant's reflections on the transition to the supersensible are written just before he begins working in earnest on the *Opus postumum's* transition project. There is not an overlap in content between these two sets of

---

[24] 8:389, cf. 404; on practical cognition, see Kain 2010 and Willaschek 2017: 108–9, 113–15.

[25] Reference to another transition appears in the late 1790s in the *Metaphysics of Morals* (1797), when Kant draws a parallel between the transition from the metaphysical foundations to physics – the project of the *Opus postumum* – and the transition from the metaphysics of morals to the "application of the pure principles of duty to cases of experience" (6: 468, cf. 6: 216–17). Louden (2000: 185 n.12) points out that this analogous practical transition is not discussed in the *Opus postumum*. Thorndike (2018) attempts to connect these two transition projects.

writings on 'transitions,' at least not with the *Opus postumum* drafts written before 1800. It is true that in the final drafts, fascicle I of December 1800 to February 1803, Kant does return to the notion of a transition to the supersensible in the guise of a "system of ideas" (e.g. 21:38) or a "transition to the limit of all knowledge – God and the world" (21:9), proposing that "the concept of freedom makes the connection [*Verband*] of the transition" (21:46).[26] But, in the main, the *Opus postumum* drafts are concerned with the *opposite* of a transition to the supersensible, where the latter is a realm of pure thought beyond experience.[27] By far the most common description that Kant uses for his project in the *Opus postumum* is the *transition from the metaphysical foundations of natural science to physics*. This is usually abbreviated along the lines of "Übergang von den metaph. A. Gr. der N.W. zur Physik." This transition aims at physics, the science of physical bodies.

The first appearance of the term 'transition' in the drafts is also the first time that Kant describes his project in his standard form, or almost: "Transition from the metaphysics of nature to physics" appears straightaway as a title at the top of a page (21:463, see Adickes 1920: 49).[28] The next page in this series of loose leaves dated prior to 1796 has a variation on this title, "~~Transition~~ <Overstep> from the metaphysics of corporeal nature to physics" (21:465). Despite their titles, these pages do not reflect on the concept of this transition; they instead continue the reflections in the previous loose leaves on specific properties of matter, such as rigidity, impenetrability, gravitation, cohesion, and density (see Tuschling 1971: 16–17). The earliest so-called *Oktaventwurf* drafts from 1796 continue to treat these topics; the formulation of the transition project, now in what will be its standard form, appears as the title on the first of these pages (21:373).

Kant first reflects on the transition problem in general midway through the *Oktaventwurf* drafts.[29] Although the first expression of the problem, the passage already contains many elements that will be key to Kant's subsequent reflections. Writing, as far as we know, a year after setting aside the "What Real Progress?" essay, Kant begins by reflecting on the notion of progressing (*das Fortschreiten*) in science in general. He distinguishes between a doctrine of elements and a doctrine of method – the systematic division employed in the

---

[26] I return in Sections 4.1 and 5.9 to the more complex transitions that Kant explores in the final fascicle I.

[27] Lehmann (1969: 192) also makes this point.

[28] Unless otherwise noted, the rest of this section will discuss passages from drafts dating prior to May 1799.

[29] A description appears on loose leaf 6, which Adickes includes with the loose leaves that he dates prior to 1796. However, Tuschling and Förster convincingly argue that this page does not belong here but rather with the loose leaves 3/4, 5, and 7 that Adickes dates as August to September 1798. See Tuschling 1971: 91 n.1, 125–8 and Förster's note in Kant 1993: 262-3 n.30.

first and second *Critiques* – to claim that the former identifies the elements of a science and the latter connects them into a whole (we shall see in Section 5 that these concepts are important to Kant's later reflections on the character of physics). He continues,

> The transition (*transitus*) from one kind of knowledge to another must only be a step (*paßus*), not a leap (*saltus*), that is, the doctrine of method requires one to *step over* [*überzuschreiten*] from the metaphysical foundations of natural science to physics, from concepts of nature that are given a priori to empirical ones that provide an empirical cognition: the rule here will be (according to the joking adage of a philosopher) to make [the transition] like the elephants, who do not move one of their four feet further until they feel that the other three stand firm. (21:386–7)

This is Kant's first general statement of the transition problem. We can examine, in turn, five characteristics of the transition problem introduced here, with reference to other passages where needed.

The first characteristic is one we have already seen in Kant's earlier writings. A transition should not be a leap – no *Sprung* or *saltus* – but an *orderly* movement, a step or crossing. In later drafts from 1799–1800, Kant reprises his criticisms of a *salto mortale*, now equated with a chaotic leap from the metaphysical foundations to physics (22:279, 512). The risk of a leap, an early draft suggests, is that one knows neither where one is going nor from where one has come (21:526). Later formulations heighten the danger: the leap would be "over a gulf that is far too wide for it to be dared" (21:505).

Notably, Kant uses the term *überschreiten* in the quoted passage. *Überschritt* can signify transgression as well as transition. In the first *Critique*, the verbal form appears when Kant warns about illegitimately overstepping the boundary of reason and of possible experience, a boundary that the critical philosophy intends to secure (e.g. A296/B353, A580/B608; see Howard 2022). In the *Opus postumum*, however, Kant uses *Überschritt* and *überschreiten* affirmatively, synonymously with *transitus* and in contrast to an illegitimate leap (e.g. 21:407, 528, 641). These newly positive references to overstepping are consistent with the investigations Kant pursues in the 1790s into how to legitimately pass from one domain to a completely separate one (in that case, from the sensible to the supersensible).

The second feature of the transition problem is thus the *heterogeneity* of the domains. Numerous variations on this point appear in the *Opus postumum*. Very regularly, the transition from the metaphysical foundations to physics is depicted as a move from one *territory* to another. It is also the transition from one *system* to another (21:407), or from *one type of cognition* to another (21:387). At the beginning of a page titled "On the transition," Kant asks himself, "What is a transition from one field (*territorium*) of science to another?" He then notes that "these two fields are specifically different according to their principles" (22:242). The transition is thus between two domains that have "heterogenous principles" (21:475). Already in the passage quoted above (21:386–7), the domains are distinguished in that the metaphysical foundations contain a priori concepts, and physics contains empirical concepts. The various specific distinctions between the two domains will be examined in the next section. But in general terms Kant's point is that a transition does not imply a continuum (22:244). It is not the case, he writes, that the "boundary point" of the metaphysical foundations is "at once the beginning point" of physics (21:505). The transition cannot simply bring the heterogenous domains together; a gap or gulf will remain between them, which the transition must cross.[30] Nevertheless, the principle of continuity applies: the next point will show how.

An image that Kant does not use in the passage quoted above, but which subsequently becomes more prominent – and which will be central to my claims in Section 4 – depicts the two domains of the metaphysical foundations and physics as two banks (*Ufer*) over which a *bridge* must be thrown. This is the third notable characteristic of Kant's conception of the transition. The image of the two banks first appears in a draft of a Preface in the *Oktaventwurf* (21:403).[31] Here, Kant envisages the transition as a step from one bank to another. He later adds the image of the bridge. This addition helps clarify the "step" of the transition. As Kant puts it on a loose leaf, one cannot proceed from the metaphysics of nature to physics as if one "only needs to put one foot in front of another" because there is "a gulf over which philosophy must throw a bridge in order to reach the opposite bank" (21:475). The transition may be conceived of as a step, but it is not only that, because the two banks represent completely different orders of principles and there is a *Kluft* or *Lücke* between them.

Before one "lifts one's foot" to start making the transition, then, "one first needs to reflect on whether it should be step or a leap, or whether on the contrary a causeway [*Fußsteig*] or a bridge between must be laid out" (21:179–80). Perhaps to emphasize this point, Kant suggests that the transition is *not* a step, but a bridge: "Between metaphysics and physics is still a wide gulf (*hiatus in systemato*) where the transition is made not through a step but

---

[30] Kant's very first mention of the "gap" between the metaphysical foundations and physics in the drafts does suggest that it must be "filled" (*ausfüllen, Ausfüllung*) (21:482). But his subsequent references to the gap move away from this image to that of bridging a divide that remains.

[31] An earlier reference to "banks" appears in the context of Kant denying that a transition from mechanical to organic nature can be made: this must be a "leap" because "for us, no bridge is laid across from one bank to reach the other" (21:388).

through a bridge of intermediary concepts, which constitute a special structure [*ein besonderes Bauwerk*]" (21:476). Elsewhere, this image of a special construction is embellished: the transition proceeds via a bridge that demands "a special extension [*Anbau*] (of pillars and arches)" (21:641).[32] The transition is a bridge between two banks, across a gulf or gap that can neither be stepped nor leaped over.

Kant's insistence that the transition is thought of as a bridge linking two banks tends to be accompanied, as in the passage just quoted, by the notion of *intermediary* or *mediating* concepts (*Zwischenbegriffe, Mittelbegriffe*), the fourth characteristic of the transition problem that I wish to highlight. Section 4 will examine these intermediary concepts in more detail. Kant defines them in the abstract as concepts "given in one [territory] and applied in the other" and which "belong as much to one territory as the other" (21:525). This definition suggests that intermediary concepts have a bridging role because they are taken from one "bank" and are applied on the other. From which science are the intermediary concepts taken and in which are they applied? An early draft immediately following the *Oktaventwurf* depicts mediating concepts as "the application of a priori concepts to experience in general" and notes their proximity to the "principles of possibility of experience in general" set out in the first *Critique* (21:311).[33] On this picture, the intermediary concepts would simply be metaphysical or transcendental concepts that are applied or realized in physics. However, as we shall see in Section 4.2, the situation turns out to be more complex than this: the intermediary concepts can also be drawn from physics and applied in metaphysics. Kant's more developed view is that intermediary concepts "can participate [*Antheil haben können*]" in the two banks that they connect (21:475). They are intermediary simply in that they relate both to the metaphysical foundations and to physics.

Finally, the fifth characteristic of the transition is that *caution* is required. This is evident in the memorable image in the first passage quoted: the philosopher seeking to make the transition should move like an elephant, only moving a foot when the other three are securely placed. A draft from September–October 1798 makes the now-standard point that the transition is neither a step through adjoining territories nor a leap, then adds that it proceeds "by means of a bridge that spans a gulf and on which one must linger, in order to step with order and according to a secure principle into the territory of physics" (21:163). The need to linger on the bridge of the transition relates to the care needed to cross from the metaphysical foundations to physics. Kant notes that the transition is "indeed not

---

[32] "[V]on Pfeilern und Bogen": Kant could be playing on the double meaning of *Bogen*, an architectural arch and a sheet of paper, with regard to his philosophical architectonic in the drafts.

[33] In fact Kant writes, tautologically, that the application should be applied: "zur Anwendung der Begriffe a priori auf Erfahrung überhaupt anzuwenden."

a dwelling [*Einwohnung*] (*incolatus*) but nevertheless a sojourn [*Aufenthalt*]"
(22:167). The science of transition is not a resting place: by this, Kant conceivably
means that it is not an end in itself but is pursued for the sake of physics, in a way
that we shall examine further in Section 5. In these passages from
September 1798, Kant already seems conscious of the difficulty of the transition.
Extending his point that the transition does not take place through a leap or
a continuum, he indicates that it must be lingered over with caution.

3.4 The Relation between the Gap and the Transition

We have identified various characteristics of the general transition problem as
Kant presents it in the drafts prior to spring 1799. Not a leap but a smooth
movement, the transition nevertheless proceeds from one domain to another,
between which there is no continuity but rather a gap or gulf. It can thus be
conceived of as a bridge from one bank to another, one that proceeds through
intermediary concepts with relations to both the departure and the arrival point,
which should bring about a careful crossing.

With these characteristics in hand, we can consider whether Kant, in the
project contained in the *Opus postumum*, primarily aims to fill a gap in his
previous thought, as the major interpretations of the past fifty years maintain.
First, some conceptual clarifications are needed. We can distinguish two main
senses of *Lücke*, which are also contained in the equivalent English term, 'gap.'
A primary meaning of *Lücke* is inadequacy or lack: something that should be
present but is missing. This meaning motivates recent debates: the gap that
commentators have searched for is a problem or failing in Kant's earlier
philosophy that must be rectified. A gap in this evaluative sense can conceivably
be envisaged as an unpaid bill that provokes a "pain like that of Tantalus."

A second meaning is more neutral: *Lücke* can signify a space between two
things, a space that is not a failing or a troublesome lack but simply a separation.
This sense of gap links it to the term in the introduction to the third *Critique*,
which Kant seems to use interchangeably with *Lücke* in the *Opus postumum*:
gulf (*Kluft*). The neutral sense of gap or gulf is evident if we think of a canyon:
we do not primarily think of canyons as problems that should be solved – for
example, by filling them in. Their existence is not a failing that must be rectified
but simply a fact: they can be found in the landscape, and we can either stop
before them and go back or build a bridge over them. Of course, a gap in
this second sense *can* be considered a gap in the first sense. If I am responsible
for maintaining a tarmacked road, the factual existence of a large crack is for me
a problem to be solved. But this only serves to underline the distinction between
the two senses of the term.

Which sense of 'gap' is at stake when Kant employs the term? As we have seen, it is key to his account that the gap between the metaphysical foundations of natural science and physics cannot be 'filled in.' The heterogeneity of the domains cannot be treated like a problem that can be rectified. The fact of the difference between the domains will remain, which is why a science of the transition is needed to bridge the two banks. At the same time, this is a task that Kant considers pressing. But does it comprise an evaluative gap in Kant's previous philosophy?

The scholarship on the gap problem tends to conflate the evaluative and neutral meanings of the term 'gap.' Kant's much-cited letters of 1798 encourage this conflation, because they mention the transition project while alluding to his "pain like that of Tantalus" and the need to "fill a gap" either in the "system of transcendental philosophy" or with regard to his "critical business." The letters seem to imply that that the neutral gap between two disciplines, which is at stake in the transition project, is an evaluative gap, and indeed one afflicting Kant's previous philosophy. I shall shortly question whether we should read the letters like this, but even if we do, these brief passages in two letters should not be given priority over hundreds of pages of the *Opus postumum*. I am not aware of a passage in the drafts that equates the gap that the transition seeks to bridge with a failing that Kant is proposing to rectify in his earlier philosophy.[34]

The interpretation I wish to propose is bolstered by a distinction made by Förster, if we push his claims further than he does. Förster (2000: 50–3) insists that that the issues of the gap and the transition are not two sides of the same problem. Based on Kant's correspondence with Kiesewetter, Förster argues that Kant is likely to have first mentioned the transition project to Kiesewetter in 1790, but the 'gap' does not appear in the *Opus postumum* or Kant's letters until 1798.

---

[34] Förster (2000: 52–3) notes that the first references to the 'gap' in the *Opus postumum* appear on the loose leaves of August–September 1798 (fourth fascicle). But the references are only to the gap or gulf between the metaphysical foundations and physics (21:482, 475, 476). Förster (2000: 188 n.23) adds that the gap is later mentioned several times, particularly on the "Farrago" sheets: 21:626, 637, 640, 642; 22:182. The passages refer to the standard gap between the metaphysical foundations and physics, with two exceptions: these refer to filling a gap "in the pure doctrine of nature and generally in the system of a priori principles" (21:626) and "in the system of pure natural science (*philosophia naturalis pura*)"; this will "close the circle of everything that belongs to the a priori cognition of nature" (21:640). Friedman (1992: 214–15) cites these two passages, but he omits "of nature" from the latter, which enables him to claim that the passage is referring to "the critical system as a whole" rather than to pure natural science. A third passage refers to the "filling of a gap," without specifying which gap (22:182). These three passages interestingly refer to 'gap' in the sense of 'lack.' But, as in the letters to Garve and Kiesewetter, to which I shall shortly return, these are gaps in the wider system of philosophy and the doctrine of nature, not in the previously published critical works. None of the passages that Förster quotes from the *Opus postumum*, then, refer to a gap in Kant's earlier philosophy. Thorndike (2018: 31) uses the same passage as Förster (2000: 51) from 21:482 to claim that Kant's transition project addresses a gap in the critical philosophy; again, the passage does not say this.

I find this historical argument convincing.[35] But I would extend Förster's proposal. Not only is it conceivable that, for Kant, the transition project and the problem of the gap in his earlier philosophy are separate issues that struck him at different times, but this helps us to see that the evaluative gap implied in the much-cited letters is distinct from the neutral gap of the transition project.[36] I would therefore follow Förster's first step of separating the 'transition' from the 'gap' (in the sense of a problem in Kant's earlier philosophy), but not his second step, where he nevertheless claims that the gap problem is decisive for the development of Kant's thought in the *Opus postumum*.

Moreover, even if one wishes to continue to use the 1798 letters as an interpretive key for understanding Kant's transition project – which I would not recommend – it is far from obvious that Kant is there thinking of a gap in the sense of a failing in his previous thought. A careful reading reveals that in neither letter does Kant say that his "pain like that of Tantalus" results from a problem or failing that needs to be rectified in his *published critical* works. The letter to Garve describes a gap in the "system of transcendental philosophy," and Kant refers to his not yet fully settled account regarding "the whole of philosophy." The system of transcendental philosophy is clearly broader than the critical propaedeutic to that system, and Kant would surely not have mistaken his critical writings for the whole of philosophy. Similarly, in the letter to Kiesewetter, Kant presents the transition-science as part of *philosophia naturalis* and writes that the "system" should not lack this part (cf. A845–6/ B873–4). It is true that he tells Kiesewetter that he wishes to "conclude his critical business and fill a gap that still remains." But even this suggestion that the transition project is the concluding part of the critical philosophy does not imply an evaluative gap *in* the critical philosophy: the gap can still be, as the *Opus postumum* drafts themselves suggest, the new task of the transition from the metaphysical foundations to physics.

Early *Opus postumum* interpreters read the relation between the transition and the gap in the way that I am proposing. When they mention the 1798 letters, Adickes (1920: iv, 2, 158–62), de Vleeschauwer (1937: 567–8), and Lehmann (1969: 192, 275) describe the transition project as a new effort to bridge the domains of the metaphysics of nature and empirical physics. For them, 'gap' does not mean a failing in the earlier works.[37] These commentators' support for

---

[35] Edwards (2008: 236–7) is nevertheless correct to say that Förster's conjectural reconstruction does not definitively prove anything.

[36] Indeed, the distinction I wish to make can be found hidden in a footnote in Förster's (2003: 238 n.5) reply to his critics.

[37] Similarly, Mathieu (1989: 39) straightforwardly considers the "gap" at stake in the drafts to be between "'metaphysics' in the Kantian sense (of the *MFNS*), and physics as science of experience."

a position does not, of course, reliably indicate its worth, but in this case I consider them to indicate a more straightforward and feasible interpretation, which recent scholarship has obscured by conflating the gap problem with the question of Kant's self-critique.

One clarification is needed. When arguing that the gap at stake in the transition project of the *Opus postumum* is not a failing in Kant's earlier philosophy, I do not intend to claim that the late drafts are entirely consistent with his previous works. I therefore do not agree with Hall's methodological principle that we should favor interpretations that make the *Opus postumum* maximally consistent with the earlier critical works (Hall 2014: 6). By contrast, I agree with Tuschling and Edwards, among others, that there are many points in the drafts where Kant at least explores diverging significantly from the positions he previously established. In my view, however, these divergences are rarely best understood as Kant's attempts to solve problems in his earlier philosophy.[38] Rather, Kant is willing to adjust his earlier positions where the problem of the transition to physics seems to demand it.

The question is therefore one of emphasis: in my view, we should avoid interpreting the *Opus postumum* from a perspective centred on the canonical critical works. While it is natural for readers to want to do this, given the historical impact of the critical philosophy and the debates that still rage over its interpretation, I consider it a mistake to think that in the period 1796–1801 Kant's primary philosophical concern was to rectify difficulties in his earlier works. The late drafts present abundant evidence of Kant's intense focus on his new projected work and its philosophical problem, namely, the transition from the metaphysical foundations of natural science to physics. Where Kant explores altering his established views, he does so in service of his attempts to solve the problem of his new transition project.

4 The Form of the Transition Problem

4.1 Stable Form, Shifting Content

The previous sections examined Kant's general conception of the transition in the early drafts of the *Opus postumum*. I shall now zoom out to consider the transition problem across the various phases of the drafts and the question of the unity or disunity of Kant's project. The key image in Kant's early accounts, I suggested, is that the transition should throw a bridge across a gulf to connect

---

[38] An exception is the circularity problem in Kant's account of density: it is well documented that this troubled Kant and spurred some of the earliest work in the drafts (see footnote 17 and the literature cited there). However, I do not think that it remains a major source of inspiration as the drafts progress. Kant's shifting concerns will be examined in what follows.

the banks on either side, a bridge that should be constituted by intermediary concepts. I propose that we should take this image to show the *stable form* of the transition problem. From the earliest to the latest drafts, Kant repeatedly formulates his problem as the attempt to make the transition from the metaphysical foundations of natural science to physics. In the final and most speculative drafts in fascicle I, written after December 1800, Kant also outlines a series of transitions that begin from the metaphysical foundations of natural science and progress through physics, transcendental philosophy, and beyond.[39] But even here, Kant's standard formulation of the problem regularly appears and is still arguably the anchor around which his reflections revolve.[40]

However, this does not mean that the problem does not change as Kant works on it. I consider it helpful to make a classical distinction, which is familiar from Kant's earlier writings and regularly appears in the late drafts, between the form and content of the problem. The form of the transition problem may be stable, but its content constantly shifts. That is, Kant incessantly rethinks the two poles of the transition problem, the metaphysical foundations of natural science and physics, as well as the means through which he attempts to make the transition. We can therefore adapt the image Kant commonly uses for his undertaking. If the transition project aims to throw a bridge between two banks, then, under the pressure of Kant's reiterated attacks on the problem, the two banks constantly shift and the materials for the bridge are ever-changing.

My proposal may be compared to Tuschling's general conception of Kant's final project. He describes the drafts as "stations of a process of reflection lasting years, which ... has its regularities but which is not fixed once and for all and which also provides no systematically determined space from which the sub-problems would be explicable" (Tuschling 1971: 11). The *Opus postumum* is *a* work insofar as it records this *process* of Kant's thinking. As Tuschling (1971: 11) puts it, "the unity of the o.p. is not static but dynamic, constituted through the continuity of the Kantian reflections; understood like this, the o.p. is in fact a single work." The dynamic unity of the drafts emerges, for Tuschling, from

---

[39] Examples of these series culminate in *dynamica generalis* (21:18); in the doctrine of freedom and physics as a system (21:61); and in the "general connection of living forces of all things in the counter-relation [*Gegenverhältnis*] God and world" (21:17). Kant sometimes replaces physics with transcendental philosophy as the destination of the transition (21:79, 85). Famously, fascicle I is concerned with the "system of ideas," which Kant describes as the "transition to the limit of all knowledge – God and the world" (21:9). Sometimes Kant states that the transition to a system of ideas takes place *after* the transition from the metaphysical foundations of natural science to physics (21:102). Elsewhere, he suggests that the standard transition takes place "through ideas"; more counterintuitively, this implies that the reflections on God and the world in fascicle I are in service of the same transition to physics as the earlier drafts (21:117).

[40] 21:15, 26, 45, 59, 116, 117, 125.

Kant's continuous process of reflection, but, as an unfinished work, there is no static unity to which the various trains of thought can be related and thus understood in a systematically related way. Tuschling thus believes that a systematically oriented interpretation of the *Opus postumum* is impossible (see Section 2).

By distinguishing between the form and content of Kant's transition project, I aim to do justice to the inherently dynamic and fluid nature of the *Opus postumum* drafts. My addition to Tuschling's useful methodological proposal is that I take Kant's dynamic "single work" to possess a greater systematic unity than Tuschling allows, because it can be viewed as organized by the consistent form of the transition problem. This stable form provides, to borrow Tuschling's terms, a "systematically determined space" that can help us to interpret Kant's very diverse reflections in the light of his general, formal transition problem.

In my view, Adickes (1897a: 53) is right to stress that Kant thought "with his pen in his hand": the drafts are a record of Kant's thought processes (see Karl 2007; Howard 2018). The drafts can in this respect be compared to the *Duisburg Nachlaß* of the 1770s, which have been described as a "philosophical laboratory" in which Kant developed many of the ideas that would appear in the *Critique of Pure Reason* (Laywine 2003: 444). The difference is, of course, that the *Opus postumum* drafts were never organized by Kant into a finished work. Borrowing a phrase from Klaus Reich, Tuschling (1971: 13) describes the *Opus postumum* as Kant's "scientific diary." I agree with Basile (2013: 362) when he notes that such a conception is unsatisfying from a strictly philosophical perspective, from which we would be interested not only in a thinker's "psychological process" but in "the logic of their thought."[41] Alongside his "diary" description, however, Tuschling (1971: 13) also calls the *Opus postumum* "the comprehensive documentation of the genesis of a Kantian work (which admittedly was never completed)." This part of Tuschling's description chimes with my approach to the *Opus postumum*. The *idea* of the uncompleted "work" that would achieve the transition allows us to unify Kant's varied philosophical experiments as a series of attempts to grapple with a single, albeit merely formal, problem.

The reader may still worry that my interpretative proposal furnishes the late drafts with only a very minimal stability and unity. I would agree, and I do not believe that we can do more than this. The *Opus postumum* is an unfinished work: we do not know how Kant would have worked up the drafts into his

---

[41] An alternative challenge is offered by Helbig (2020: 69, 71) who provocatively suggests that we should *avoid* "the teleological temptation to see layers of drafts as nothing but preliminaries to a work that happens, in the case of the O.p., to remain unfinished"; instead, we could view the drafts as "a writing constellation."

envisaged publication, nor whether they are anywhere near completion. This means that the *Opus postumum* is of interest less for its philosophical results, which are always tentative and constantly revised throughout the drafts, than for the way it shows Kant in the process of thinking and creatively attempting to solve problems.

4.2 The Elements of the Transition Problem

Of the three elements of the formal transition problem – the two banks and the bridge – it is striking that scholarship has considered the transition almost exclusively through the *departure* point, the 'metaphysical foundations.' What is this departure point? Different commentators have argued that the transition project emerges primarily from the *Metaphysical Foundations of Natural Science*, the *Critique of Judgment*, and the *Critique of Pure Reason*, and with regard to various problems in these works (see Section 3.1). In these debates, the work and topic presented as the target of Kant's self-critique often equates to how commentators understand the 'metaphysical foundations' from which the transition departs.

It is generally agreed that when Kant writes "metaph. A. Gr. der N.W." in his formulations of the problem, we should not take him to be referring in any straightforward sense to the short work of the same title published in 1786. Tuschling makes this point in the course of arguing that Kant's drafts are primarily a self-critique targeted at his 1786 work, after which "nothing remains but the Phoronomy" (Tuschling 1971: 117). We need not commit to what Mathieu (1989: 50) calls Tuschling's "extraordinarily bold" overall thesis, but we can follow Tuschling in recognizing that the phrase "metaphysical foundations of natural science" in Kant's formulation of the transition problem does not straightforwardly align with the published *Metaphysical Foundations of Natural Science*.[42]

I consider Emundts (2004) to give a convincing account of Kant's *initial* motivation to embark on the transition project. Kant sought to better address the problem at stake in the General Remark to the Dynamics chapter of the *Metaphysical Foundations*, namely, to "completely present" what he calls the "moments" to which the "specific variety" of matter must be able to be brought a priori (4:525). In 1786, Kant tentatively "hopes" that he has accomplished this complete presentation of the variety of types of matter. He thus explains the properties of density, cohesion, elasticity, and chemical dissolution on the basis of the two fundamental physical forces (4:525–32; see Emundts 2004: 48–54; Thorndike 2018: 51–65). Early pages of the *Opus postumum* drafts attempt to

---

[42] Förster (2000: 180 n.23) also expresses skepticism about Tuschling's "radical thesis."

explain and classify a wider range of material properties, including ponderability (being weighable), fluidity, and crystallization. On the reading of Emundts (2004: 67–73), Kant starts to seek not only to further develop but to replace the 1786 General Remark. But this task becomes significantly more complicated when, in 1792, Kant becomes aware of the circularity problem afflicting his theory of matter.[43] In this endeavor, the proof of the existence of the ether takes a newly central place.

The ether, which Kant also calls caloric, thus becomes, by May 1799, the intermediary concept par excellence.[44] Caloric is the posited material substance that scientists including Lavoisier thought necessary for explaining heat (see Adickes 1922: 329–51). Previously, Kant had explored whether the empirical properties of matter, such as ponderability, could serve as the intermediary concepts for the transition.[45] The growing significance of the concept of caloric is evident in the Elementary System drafts of October 1798 to May 1799. Kant explains fluidity and rigidity on the basis of caloric in the Elementary System drafts, then starts to conceive of it as a concept that can be given empirically but known a priori (Emundts 2004: 136–40; Förster 2000: 15–16). The subsequent attempted proofs of caloric or the ether have been extensively discussed in the literature, particularly in recent decades.[46]

I stress that Emundts' account accurately characterizes Kant's *initial* motivation because, in my view, his project radically develops as he works on it. This means that the initial problems – the development of the General Remark to the Dynamics and the circularity in his account of density – become supplemented or even replaced by other concerns. The major shift, in my view, takes place with regard to Kant's conception of physics in fascicles X/XI.

5 What Is Physics?

5.1 The Arrival Point of the Transition

If we understand Kant's unfinished final project through his image of throwing a bridge between two banks, it is striking, as I have noted, how heavily the scholarship has focused on the *departure point* of the transition, the metaphysical foundations of natural science. Remarkably little attention has been given to

---

[43] Again, this is the problem that, on the theory of the *Metaphysical Foundations*, the density of a body seems to depend on the degree of its attractive force, and the degree of attractive force depends on the density. See footnote 17 above.

[44] Regarding Kant's indifference to the terminology, see for example 21:218 and 22:331, cited by Hall (2015: 71) and Mathieu (1989: 136).

[45] On ponderability (*ponderabilitas*, *Wägbarkeit*), the property of being weighable, see Förster 2000: 16–18.

[46] Mathieu 1989: 111–27; Edwards 2000: 152–66; Förster 2000: 82–101; Emundts 2004: 156–201; Hall 2015: 93–122; Rollman 2015.

the transition's *arrival point*: Kant's conception of physics in the drafts. In the rest of this Element, I aim to go some way toward rectifying this situation and to encourage more work on the relevant phase of the drafts.

It is in fascicles X/XI of August 1799 to April 1800 that Kant is most intensely concerned with how to conceptualize physics. As noted in Section 2, the major studies since 1970 pay little attention to these drafts. By contrast, Adickes, de Vleeschauwer, and Lehmann place fascicles X/XI at the centre of their interpretations. But, I argued, their discussions of the so-called 'new deduction' in fascicles X/XI are particularly egregious examples of their imposition of external philosophical concerns onto the drafts.

Kant wrote most of the *Opus postumum* on large sheets of paper folded once to make a 'folio' of four sides. In fascicles X/XI, he is in the habit of designating each folio with a sequential letter. The drafts of this period, designated A to Z, then AA and BB, therefore constitute twenty-five attempts to develop a part of the transition project.[47] As we can be confident about the order of these drafts, they provide particular insight into the development of Kant's thinking. But the importance of these drafts is not limited to this. I have argued elsewhere that fascicles X/XI can be seen as the "transition within the transition" because they stand between two phases that have received more attention in the scholarship, the ether proofs and the *Selbstsetzungslehre* (Howard 2019). Their intermediary character is not only chronological: I have suggested that fascicles X/XI take up important resources from the drafts that bookend them, namely, the ether as a material condition of experience and the "first act" of the subject in positing itself in space and time. The two issues – the proof of the ether and what has been called Kant's *Selbstsetzungslehre* – can be considered objective and subjective approaches, respectively, to the transition problem. There is evidence in fascicles X/XI of Kant attempting to connect these two approaches (see Howard 2019: 608–16). I shall not repeat this argument here. Instead, I shall explore a central issue of the 1799–1800 drafts: how physics can be conceived of as a *system*.

The limitations in the existing scholarship on fascicles X/XI are evident in Basile's (2013: 411–20) systematic summary of work on this phase of the drafts. Basile discusses four issues: the 'new deduction,' self-affection, the appearance of the appearance, and the embodied subject. We shall return to some of these topics. Here, we need note only that Basile presents all four issues in terms of opposed idealist and realist interpretations. The impression from Basile's discussion of the existing literature is that these drafts merely

---

[47] As was customary at the time when alphabetizing lists, letters J and V are not used. Kant has both a BB and BB[2], but the latter is on the third page of the same folio, so I have counted BB and BB[2] as a single attempt (22:448).

lead to aporia.[48] Basile's summary does not mention the question that Kant continually asks himself in fascicles X/XI: "What is physics?"

5.2 Prevailing Views on the Conception of Physics in the *Opus postumum*

Why has Kant's conception of physics, the arrival point of the transition, received so little attention? No doubt because it has been taken to be straightforward and unproblematic. Hoppe's book is still the main study of this issue in the *Opus postumum*. Appropriately, it foregrounds fascicles X/XI: it is here that Hoppe (1969: 115) considers the transition to physics, strictly speaking, to take place. For him, the primary question at stake in the *Opus postumum* is the transcendental one of the possibility of physics. But he presents Kant's conception of physics in very narrow terms. After citing a passage in which Kant asks, reprising the form of the questions in the *Prolegomena*, "How is science of experience (physics) in general possible?" (22:331), Hoppe (1969: 94) tellingly adds: "that means of course, how are experiments possible?" Physics in the *Opus postumum*, on Hoppe's view, is an empirical science of observation and experiment. After citing various passages in which Kant describes physics in these terms, Hoppe (1969: 88) states, "the question of the transition is therefore how physics, which is designated in this way as experimental natural science or experimental research into nature, is possible." The transcendental question would thus ultimately be the question of the conditions of possibility of physical experiments (Hoppe 1969: 117). On this view, Kant does not merely describe the experimental procedure of physics but "rather wants to show *how* an objective empirical cognition of nature *through experiment* is possible" (Hoppe 1969: 137, second emphasis mine).

On Hoppe's reading, physics is conceived of throughout the *Opus postumum* as an observational and experimental doctrine of nature. The range of concepts that Kant introduces in the drafts – particularly, the mediating concepts and the notions of *Hineinlegen*, the appearance of the appearance, self-affection, and *forma dat esse rei*[49] – are, for Hoppe, conditions of possibility of experiments: experiment-ideas (*Versuchsideen*) (Hoppe 1969: 97). They are merely formal constructs for the sake of experimental physics. It cannot be denied that there are passages that support this reading (for examples, see Hoppe 1969: 87–8). But Hoppe's interpretation is forced because he must ignore the numerous

---

[48] An exception, which Basile does not mention in his systematic summary, is Caygill's (2005) discussion of Kant's investigation of physics in fascicle XI, which identifies a number of the issues that I examine more closely in what follows.

[49] We shall return to these concepts in Sections 5.7 and 5.8, with the exception of the "appearance of the appearance": for discussion of this, see Hoppe 1969: 118–22 and Mathieu 1989: 144–53.

passages, to which we turn in the remaining sections, in which Kant defines physics very differently.

Although it is not regularly cited, the spirit of Hoppe's account of physics in the *Opus postumum* lives on in some subsequent interpretations. Emundts (2004: 1) sets out from the view that physics, in the *Opus postumum*, is simply an empirical science. She does insist on the importance of systematicity for the transition project. However, this systematicity is said not to be intrinsic to physics but furnished by the transition: "The task of a system *established for* empirical physics consists in systematically analysing the specific variety of matter, so that a plan of all possible moving forces can be established" (Emundts 2004: 119, my emphasis). The transition provides a systematic basis for physics, but the latter remains defined by its experimental and observational procedure.[50]

I agree that this restricted conception of physics predominates in the drafts in the period examined by Emundts (that is, before August 1799). However, in the subsequent fascicles X/XI, Kant reflects intensively on the nature of physics and whether it is *itself* systematic. The emergence of different conceptions of physics after August 1799 is significant, in my view, because Kant seems to foresee and arguably forestalls objections that commentators later target at the very idea of his transition project. Tuschling, for instance, ends his study by dismissing the fundamental problem with which Kant was concerned in the drafts:

> The ventures that Kant undertook under the title of a transition thus end paradoxically with the knowledge that a continuous transition from the metaphysics of nature to physics is impossible: the domain, object and method of metaphysical dynamics, on the one hand, and of physics, on the other, are separated from one another by a fundamental [*prinzipielle*] boundary. ... Physics is and remains empirical science, its objects are given in empirical intuition, its method is the development of hypotheses and their testing through empirical observation and experiment. – Across this 'gulf' leads no bridge, no transition. (Tuschling 1971: 178)

Tuschling contends, like Hoppe, that physics is nothing more than an empirical science that proceeds through observation and experiment. On this basis, his concluding note dismisses the central aim of the *Opus postumum*, or the transition problem in its basic form.

The most striking example of such a dismissive conclusion appears in Adickes' book. Kant's task, Adickes writes, is "to determine the *necessary*

---

[50] See also Emundts 2004: 11. Hoppe (1969: 72–7) has a comparable interpretation of the systematicity of physics.

conditions required for the connection of both sciences [that is, the metaphysical foundations of natural science and physics], which otherwise remain separated" (Adickes 1920: 162). He continues, "To determine this necessity, and thereby the proof that the new science of 'transition' would provide an indispensable contribution to transcendental philosophy, Kant dedicated much time and work – but he also wasted this, for all the effort was in vain, because the aim towards which he strived was a mere mirage [*Fata morgana*]" (Adickes 1920: 162).

Why was Kant's final project ultimately nothing but a waste of time? Because, Adickes claims, Kant's attempt to systematize physics, so that it is not a mere aggregate, has been shown by modern physics to be futile:

> Physics remains *science* even as aggregate, if it only strictly adheres to the rules of scientific methodology in experimentation and determination of facts, as well as in its conclusions, interpretations, theories, and hypotheses. The system forms neither the beginning of the path [of physics] nor a turning point upon it but stands as the strived-for but never-attained aim at its end.
>
> (Adickes 1920: 362)

The scientific status of modern physics results from its methodology, Adickes asserts, so Kant's concern with a priori structures is irrelevant. To the modern natural scientist, "the Kantian striving after aprioricity, at least in the form that it assumes in the Op. p., appears as a useless, because fruitless, squandering of time and effort" (Adickes 1920: 362).

Adickes and Tuschling both consider it impossible to bridge the gap between the a priori metaphysics of nature and empirical physics, because the arrival point, physics, is an empirical science of observation and experiment. It treats an infinite diversity of physical phenomena that are simply given and so cannot be determined in advance. Physics thus remains a fragmentary aggregate whose subject matter can have no a priori systematic structure.[51] I believe that Adickes and Tuschling would be justified in rejecting the transition problem as a whole only *if* Kant had held their restricted conception of physics as nothing but an empirical science of observation and experiment. But fascicles X/XI show Kant engaging with precisely the problem that Adickes and Tuschling take to be an unavoidable stumbling block for the transition project: he reconsiders the kind of narrow conception of physics to which they are committed.

---

[51] Adickes and Tuschling do not take Hoppe's path to resolve this issue: they do not, in my view quite rightly, selectively read the drafts in order to claim that Kant intends only to present the merely formal a priori structures of physics. I return to the question of the formal and material "anticipation" of physics in Section 5.8.

5.3 What Is Physics? Initial Explorations

It is well known that in the final phase of the drafts, Kant provides over 150 definitions of 'transcendental philosophy' (see Adickes 1920: 149; Hall 2015: 5). Commentators have not noted, though, that fascicles X/XI contain a comparable number of attempts to define physics. Many of the pages in this period begin with the title "What is physics?" or with a definition of physics; this is then elaborated upon or revised in the main text and the margins.

An idea of the way that Kant defines and redefines physics can be gained from the folio that he designates 'A,' the first in the series that constitutes most of fascicles X/XI. Kant begins the page by giving four definitions of physics in a row.[52] These appear successively in the main text in the same ink and hand, so he is here not reworking a single definition so much as setting out expansions of or variations on his conception of physics. The definitions run as follows (numbers are mine):

[1] Physics is systematic investigation of nature through empirically given forces of matter insofar as they are connected to each other in a system.

[2] Physics is science of experience of the sum total (*complexus*) of moving forces of matter. These forces also affect the subject, the human, and its organs, because the human is also a corporeal being. The inner changes, with consciousness, that are thereby produced in [the human] are perceptions: the reaction on matter and outer changes of the latter is motion.

[3] Physics is a system of the empirical investigation of nature that [can] only take place through observation or experiment, in the first case where the object moves the physicist, in the second where the physicist moves the object and shifts it into another state of perception.

[4] Since physics is a system, but we cannot cognize a system as such, only insofar as we ourselves insert [*hineinlegen*] the manifold of an aggregate according to principles a priori and assemble it ourselves, which takes place through the concept of motion, so the division of the study of nature [*Naturkunde*] in physics, as concerns the highest division, the topic of moving forces according to the subsequent system, is analytically ~~establish~~ <sought out, [to] synthetically present>. (22:298–9)

In some respects, these definitions justify the standard view that Kant conceives of physics as simply an empirical science of observation of, and experimentation

---

[52] This is the reverse side of the half-sheet; the front, under 'A,' mainly discusses smallpox vaccination, as does the first page of 'B.' Förster notes that these reflections on vaccination are spurred by a letter Kant received about a passage on the topic in the *Metaphysics of Morals* (12:283–4, 6:424; Kant 1993: 269 n.63).

upon, nature. Definition (3) indeed states that such empirical investigation can "only take place through observation or experiment." Physics is a "science of experience" (definition 2), of "empirically given forces of matter" (definition 1).

However, Kant's emphasis on the systematicity of physics is striking. Definitions (1), (3), and (4) define physics as a system; (1) refers twice in one sentence to the systematicity of physics. These definitions do not present physics as the observational and experimental aggregation of facts for which *the transition provides* systematic unity; Kant instead suggests that physics *itself* is systematic. In (4), he adds, in elliptical terms that are not yet comprehensible, that cognition of a system requires that we "insert" the manifold ourselves by way of motion as a concept. The terse sentence that follows refers to a hierarchy of divisions in physics and alludes to a division between analytic and synthetic methods with regard to these divisions.

Furthermore, Kant's account of observation and experiment in (3) is strange. Experimentation is where "the physicist moves the object," which seems straightforward enough, but Kant adds that the physicist shifts it to "another state of perception," rather than simply another physical location. Perception was introduced in (2) as "inner changes, with consciousness." Kant is thus concerned not simply with what he calls the "outer" movements of physical bodies but also with changes in inner states of the subject. Whereas the *Metaphysical Foundations* were concerned with objects of outer sense (4:476), the language in definitions (2) and (3) suggest Kant is also considering inner sense: we shall see that subsequent drafts confirm this. Observation is then described as the process through which "the object moves the physicist." This could be understood as simply the affection of the outer senses by the physical object. However, (2) indicates an unusual kind of action and reaction, where the human is one corporeal body among others. This is of course true, but the embodiment of the scientist-subject was not usually a concern of classical physics. Moreover, Kant suggests that outer motion and inner perceptions are counterparts of each other, where outer changes in physical bodies are somehow "reactions" to the inner changes of the perceiving human.

In these four definitions at the beginning of fascicles X/XI, the concept of physics seems to have already been pulled in unfamiliar directions. Problems to which Kant alludes here will intensify as the drafts in this period progress. In Sections 5.4, 5.5, 5.6, and 5.7, we will address in turn the points that have emerged in draft 'A': the question of the systematicity of physics; the introduction of inner sense and thus the wider "physiological" sense of physics; and the reconsideration of action and reaction in terms of the moving forces of the object *and* the subject.

5.4 Elementary System

To understand Kant's investigations into the systematicity of physics, we can begin by considering his references to different kinds of system.[53] Fascicles X/XI regularly refer to the "elementary system." This must be seen in the context of the drafts of October 1798 to May 1799, which are often titled "Elem. Syst." In these drafts, Kant more systematically develops the *Oktaventwurf*'s reflections on the various specific properties of matter.[54] The 1798–9 Elementary System drafts regularly begin by noting that the properties of matter should be classified according to the four classes of the categories. In this they follow the *Metaphysical Foundations*, where Kant noted in the Preface that "the schema for completeness of a metaphysical system, whether it be of nature in general, or of corporeal nature in particular, is the table of categories" (4:473–4). Very similar phrasing appears in the Elementary System drafts: "The elementary concepts, insofar as they should lead to a system a priori, can set out nothing other than [the system] of the *categories* as the schema . . . . The division must be carried out according to the system of the categories, so through the concepts of quantity, quality, relation and modality" (22:155). Kant repeatedly runs through the four classes of the categories in his attempt to exhaustively classify physical properties such as weight, heat, cohesion, fluidity, and solidity. The aim, as an earlier loose leaf from August to September 1798 puts it, is to "classify the moving forces a priori from concepts and thus completely enumerate the properties of matter prior to experience" (21:477). Such a *complete* enumeration is an ambitious task, to say the least.

Förster (2000: 13–19) provides a good account of Kant's ultimately fruitless early classificatory endeavors.[55] Over this period, the concept of "caloric" gains ever greater prominence until it becomes *the* intermediary concept (see Section 4.2). This leads to what is often seen as a decisive turn in the drafts: Kant starts to attempt a priori proofs of the concept of caloric or the ether in the *Übergang 1–14* drafts of May–August 1799. One outcome of the troubled classificatory attempts in the Elementary System drafts, then, is Kant's recognition that the concept of caloric can serve as an intermediary concept, a material transcendental condition of experience, the hypothetical or actual existence of which should be proved. But what becomes of his notion of an elementary system, which would classify all moving forces and properties of

---

[53] This section, and Sections 5.5 and 5.6, develop ideas sketched in Howard (2023).

[54] For Kant's first references to the 'elementary system,' see Tuschling 1971: 142 n.9.

[55] For further detail, see Adickes 1920: 474–591; Tuschling 1971: 23–7, 69–89, 123–78; Mathieu 1989: 86–110.

matter a priori following the guideline of the table of categories from the first *Critique*?

The difficulties with the initial classificatory attempts can already be seen in "Elem. Syst. 1" (late 1798). Here, in a series of numbered paragraphs, Kant details properties of matter under the headers of the classes of the categories. The paragraphs run, unusually, across more than one folio. Paragraphs 6–9 discuss, under "Relation," cohesion and cohesibility (in terms of moving forces and caloric), friability, ductility, and malleability (22:146–8, see Kant 1993: 48–50). Kant then adds, under a larger header, a "Critical note": "It very much seems that in this section we have stepped far beyond the boundaries of the a priori concepts of the moving forces of matter, which should for themselves form a system, and have drifted into physics as an empirical science (e.g. into chemistry); but one will surely notice that [*breaks off*]" (22:149). It is telling that Kant's self-critical note breaks off, apparently unable to defend the proximity of these classificatory endeavors to empirical physics itself. This is a problem because empirical physics is a mere aggregate of findings and not a system.

A little earlier, in drafts of August to September 1798, Kant began to insist on the nonsystematic character of empirical physics and thus the need for the transition to systematize its results. An early draft of a preface to the projected transition work states, "Philosophical treatments do not deserve the name of philosophy as science unless they are presented as combined in a *system*" (21:524). The loose leaves 3/4, 5, 6, and 7, from the same period, attempt a series of drafts for a preface. Kant repeatedly claims that, without the transition, physics would remain fragmentary, a "mere aggregate" or "farrago."[56] In this period, he introduces some vivid language that he will reprise in fascicles X/XI: empirical physics is a mere "scrabbling-together" (*Stoppelung*) of results; and a system cannot be "knocked together" (*gezimmert*) from merely empirical concepts.[57]

The point is clearly expressed on loose leaf 6: "Merely empirical natural science can never constitute a system but at best only a fragmentary, ever-growing aggregate." Kant adds: "The moving forces of nature are not completely known to us" (21:474). There is evidently a tension between this recognition that the results of physics cannot be grasped a priori and Kant's simultaneous attempt

---

[56] See Tuschling 1971: 124. Blomme (2015: 114–20) collects passages from 1795 onward in which Kant insists that natural investigation must be systematic.

[57] For example, 21:285, 161; see Hoppe 1969: 77. *Stoppelung/stoppeln* can be translated as compilation/compile; Kant sometimes adds the Latin *compilando* or *compilatio* in parentheses. However, his term is more picturesque: *stoppeln* in an agricultural sense means to glean, to gather leftover wheat after a harvest. *Zimmern* means both to carpenter and to cobble together; Kant uses it both neutrally and (increasingly, it seems, as the drafts progress) pejoratively.

to fully enumerate and classify a priori all moving forces and physical properties in an elementary system. This tension plays out in the varying depictions of whether the transition can aspire to delimiting physics. At times, Kant suggests that physics should gain "secure boundaries or outline" through the transition (21:478); at others, he claims that physics does not have "a determinate extent and content" and implies that it cannot (21:475). We shall see this issue return in fascicles X/XI in the question of how far the results of physics can be "anticipated."

In a couple of places, most notably in an "A–B Übergang" draft of January to February 1799, Kant suggests that physics is an "empirical system" (22:240).[58] This is a strange definition because, as noted in Section 1, Kant conceives of a system as the unification and coordination of manifold cognitions under an idea a priori – not a posteriori (A832/B860, cf. A645/B673). Kant seems to recognize the oddity of his definition at this point in the *Opus postumum*: he adds that the empirical system of physics is a *"problematic* whole" of the moving forces of matter (22:240, my emphasis).

When Kant returns to the notion of an elementary system in fascicles X/XI, he insists, directly counter to his suggestion in early 1799, that the notion of an empirical system is a contradiction in terms. Indeed, he repeats this point with mantra-like regularity.[59] And if the elementary system seeks to exhaustively classify specific physical properties, it seems uncomfortably close to what Kant now insists is the contradictory notion of an empirical system. There is thus reason to wonder whether the elementary system envisaged in the early *Opus postumum* drafts is, on Kant's strict conception, a system at all. These issues underpin what I shall argue is a self-critical revision, in the 1799–1800 drafts, of his earlier notion of an elementary system.

5.5 Doctrinal and Elementary Systems in Fascicles X/XI

Across the varying definitions in fascicles X/XI, physics is most frequently designated as a doctrinal system (*Lehrsystem* or *Doctrinalsystem*), often with the Latin *systema doctrinale* in parentheses. In earlier drafts, Kant seems to use 'doctrinal system' and 'elementary system' interchangeably.[60] Fascicles X/XI, however,

---

[58] After asking himself how "a formal elementary system from mere concepts" is possible, Kant adds the title "Physics" in the middle of the page, followed by the passage I discuss. See also 21:212 (May–August 1799).

[59] For example, 22: 310, 328, 336, 345, 381, 384, 391, 395, 398, 448. Hoppe (1969: 77) cites further passages.

[60] At some points, 'doctrinal system' takes the place usually occupied by 'elementary system': 21:483, 627, 22:174; elsewhere, the two systems are explicitly equated: 22:197.

distinguish between these two systems. Draft 'G' states that "the moving forces of matter . . . form an *elementary system*, which is, indeed, the object of physics. The latter is the *doctrinal system* of the moving forces" (22:342). Physics is here a doctrinal system that has the elementary system as its *object*. Draft 'K' adds more detail:

> the moving forces can and must [be enumerated] in an elementary system of the same, which belongs to physics; and these forces, when their form is thought in view of their connection according to principles, constitute physics itself as their doctrinal system" (22:358).[61]

The elementary system, which outlines and classifies the moving forces, belongs to the doctrinal system. The doctrinal system has the same subject matter, but it adds the *form* through which the moving forces are classified and the *principles* of this form (Kant's terminology here recalls his 1770 *Dissertation*). The doctrinal system includes further reflection on the philosophical grounds of the elementary system that it contains.

Kant here suggests that the elementary system belongs to and is produced by physics. Because physics is the point at which the transition should *arrive*, it is now less clear than in the 1798–9 drafts that the elementary system forms the first part, or even any part at all, of the transition. The status of the elementary system thus apparently changes in fascicles X/XI. I take this to result from the difficulties we have seen afflict the very notion of an elementary system, which is intended to somehow exhaustively enumerate and classify the endless diversity of physical forces and properties.

This changing status of the elementary system is evident when Kant compares it to a Linnaean 'natural system.' A number of definitions of physics in fascicles X/XI distinguish between subjective and objective parts of physics. The subjective part – also called the formal or doctrinal part of physics – "can (and should) be presented completely." The objective, material, classificatory part "can never be wholly completed" (22:496, cf. 485, 498). In this passage, Kant calls the objective part of physics the natural system, and notes that an example is Carl Linnaeus' system of botanical and zoological classification.[62] In draft 'S,' immediately after defining physics as "a doctrinal system of the connection of the perception of sense objects to the formal unity of experience in the subject," Kant writes: "To the doctrinal system there corresponds, as concerns the aggregate of objects given to the senses, the natural system: – With regard to [the natural system], as whole of the coordination of natural things,

---

[61] I follow Förster and Rosen's insertion of "be enumerated" in Kant 1993: 116.
[62] 22:496. Linnaeus' *Systema Naturae* first appeared in 1735 and went through thirteen editions by 1793.

according to the principles of the division of objects of experience into classes, genera, species etc., in an elementary system of objects" (22:460; cf. 22:334–5). Here, the natural system, a classificatory system in the Linnaean mold, is distinguished from the doctrinal system (physics) and explicitly equated with the elementary system.

Kant's evaluation of the Linnaean natural system vacillates in the *Opus postumum*, just as it does elsewhere in his work (see Marcucci 2001; Emundts 2004: 54–5, 59–65). At times, he claims that it constitutes "merely methodically aggregated objects of experience"; he names it a *systema physices artificiali* (22:498). Here, Kant follows Buffon's critique of Linnaeus' classifications as arbitrary and lacking a principle.[63] Elsewhere, he claims that the Linnaean system is *not* artificial: no mere aggregate or farrago (22:342). But it seems that Kant's dismissive characterization of the Linnaean system as an unprincipled aggregate is tied up with his deepening doubts about the classificatory endeavors of his own earlier elementary system. I read such self-criticism in draft 'G':

> We cannot, it seems, even through all [our] means of making an experience, discern a priori with general validity which and how many objects of perception (which together add up to *matter*) and moving forces there are, according to type and number, which we could perhaps lay under our possible experience. Rather, [we can] at best scrappily [*stoppelnd*] enumerate certain forces by groping around [*Herumtappen*] among outer sense objects, for example hardness, softness, weight, lightness and so on, which together constitute no completed system of these forces [and] thus also the materials that they contain in themselves, because we cannot bring them to our cognition according to a principle a priori through the investigation of nature, that is, we cannot specify the fundamental materials of the moving forces nor establish an elementary system of them. (22:344)[64]

Kant here suggests that the elementary system that he had previously aimed to produce is a fragmentary "groping around." This is the phrase used in the B Preface to the first *Critique*: such groping around is the opposite of the secure scientific course pursued by the critical philosophy (Bvii, Bxi, Bxiv–xv). The passage from 'G' likewise states that fragmentary enumeration does not lead to a system, and that we therefore *cannot* establish an elementary system of the moving forces of matter.

---

[63] Marcucci 2001: 118 n.30. See also Adickes' comments on Kant's allegiance to Buffon over Linnaeus, quoted in Marcucci (2001: 121 n.37).

[64] In this passage, Kant writes of "making [*machen*] an experience," and then uses *ausmachen* in what seems to be three different ways, which I have translated as 'discern,' 'add up to,' and 'constitute.'

According to this line of Kant's thinking, the classificatory elementary system envisaged in the earlier drafts appears to be rejected entirely. Elsewhere, as noted, Kant suggests that the elementary system still belongs to the transition, but as the *object* of physics. On this more moderate view, the transition would reach physics, which then has the separate task of endlessly compiling infinitely varied empirical findings toward a systematic whole that it cannot reach, namely, the elementary or Linnean natural system. The elementary system, on this view, functions as a horizon or a regulative idea, which is how Adickes presents the system of physics in the passage quoted in Section 5.2. But Kant's position differs from Adickes' in that, for Kant, the elementary system is not the same as the doctrinal system. In fascicles X/XI, physics is predominantly defined as a doctrinal system; Kant thus apparently intends to sidestep the problems facing the notion of the elementary system, particularly its proximity to the (contradictory) notion of an empirical system.

Whether we follow Kant's radical rejection of the elementary system or his more moderate downplaying of its significance for the transition project, fascicles X/XI suggest that his conception of this task has changed by mid-1799. The elementary system is no longer the first step of the transition project but is rather a classificatory task pursued by physics once the latter science has been reached. This entails that physics is not reducible to the elementary system but is a broader endeavor. The expanded scope of physics is most evident in Kant's increased emphasis on its subjective side and his incorporation of psychology in a broader notion of 'physiology.'

5.6 Physics as Physiology

In fascicles X/XI, Kant distinguishes between the subjective part of physics, which can be completed, and the objective part, which proceeds indefinitely. As we have seen, the objective part becomes equated with the elementary system or the Linnean natural system. This then plays an increasingly minor role in Kant's conception of the transition, because it is the never-ending task of enumerating and classifying physical forces and properties, distinct from the doctrinal system that prevents physics from being an unprincipled aggregate. Given that the objective part is downplayed, it makes sense that the subjective part of physics occupies an increasingly prominent place in Kant's reflections.

A major shift in Kant's conception of the subjective part occurs when he begins to define physics as the doctrine of outer *and inner* sense objects. Here is one of many examples: physics is the "general empirical doctrine of objects of the senses (outer as well as inner) insofar as they constitute a doctrinal system"

(22:488).[65] For the reader of Kant's earlier works, this is surprising. The first *Critique* and the *Metaphysical Foundations* distinguish physics, the science of objects of outer sense, from psychology, the science of objects of inner sense (A846/B874, 4:467, 470). The distinction appears to be a fundamental one. It differentiates the two sciences with regard to what they can cognize a priori (A381) and whether their empirical doctrines can be mathematical (4:471).

However, although these works of the 1780s seem to strictly distinguish physics and psychology according to the basic distinction between outer and inner sense, they depict the two sciences as branches of a more fundamental doctrine of the objects of the senses, "physiology" (A381, A845/B873; cf. 28:222). By the time he is writing fascicles X/XI, Kant's conception of physics has broadened so that it is indistinguishable from physiology. Draft 'B' characterizes physics as "the concept of a systematic physiology" (22:307). An earlier draft (December 1798 to January 1799) proposed to rename the metaphysical foundations as "physiological foundations" (21:639). In the same period, Kant suggests that the transition might be called "a general doctrine of forces (*dynamica generalis*) or also propaedeutic physiology"; a "physiological doctrine of forces" that is the middle term in the transition.[66] Having explored conceiving of the departure point and the transition itself as physiology, then, in fascicles X/XI Kant experiments with defining the arrival point, physics, as physiology.[67]

This leads to a conception of physics as a science that treats the sum total (or complex) of not only moving forces but also *perceptions*, that is, representations accompanied by consciousness. Drafts 'S,' 'T,' 'U,' and 'X' arguably represent the high-water mark of Kant's investigations into this subjective side of physics. For example, a remarkable series of definitions opens page three of draft 'S':

> Physics is a *doctrinal system* (*systema doctrinale*) of sensible representations, insofar as they are combined through the subject's understanding into a principle of experience. – Not a fragmentary aggregate of perceptions (empirical representations with consciousness) but a system of these in the concept of the subject, according to a principle of their combination to the synthetic unity of the manifold that is given in intuition in experience. – Physics is a doctrinal system of the connection of perception of sense-objects to the formal unity of experience in the subject. (22:459–60)

---

[65] Further examples are 22:358, 407, 458, 472, 475, 482, 493, 500, 523.

[66] 21:631, 642; cf. 21:478, 22:167.

[67] Basile (2013: 283–5) notes that the psychological aspects of the transition project have been innovatively highlighted by Dario Drivet. However, Drivet's large systematic claims are unconvincing, namely, that Kant is seeking to complete the psychological part of the system of ideas, and that the transition proceeds from the *Metaphysical Foundations* to the third *Critique* and does not attempt to found empirical physics but rather medicine, the physiology of the human body. Basile (2013: 383–5) criticizes Drivet's position in more detail.

Kant's conception of physics now foregrounds the activity of the perceiving subject, who combines and unifies perceptions, outer and inner sensible representations with consciousness, into a system. On the final definition in this passage, physics is hard to distinguish from the transcendental unity of apperception in the Transcendental Deductions of the first *Critique*. Page four of the same folio proposes: "Physics is the principle for representing what is subjective in perceptions (as appearances) as objective – by means of the understanding" (22:464). It is Kant's distinction between a subjective and an objective part of physics, and his new focus on the former, that allows him to claim that physics is a doctrine that represents the subjective aspect of perceptions as objective. We are here far from Hoppe's depiction of Kant's conception of physics as an empirical doctrine that merely observes and experiments upon physical bodies, the objects of the outer senses.

5.7 Subjective Forces

Kant's train of thought takes him in a yet stranger and more intriguing direction: to speculate about the moving forces of the subject. How can the perceiving subject, as subject and not object, be said to have moving forces? To begin with, we can note that it is logical for Kant to have arrived at this point. He has distinguished between the subjective and objective sides of physics, focused on the subjective side – because only this can be completely and systematically developed – and broadened his conception of physics to equate it with physiology, a "general doctrine of forces" encompassing the objects of outer and inner sense. It is a natural step to then reflect on the activities of the subject, and to do so in terms of forces.

The turn to the activity of the subject is clearly expressed in draft 'R': "It is not in the fact that the subject is affected empirically by the object (*per receptivitatem*) but that it affects itself (*per spontaneitatem*) that there is the possibility of the transition from the metaphysical foundations of natural science to physics" (22:405). The subject's self-affection is here given a newly prominent place in the transition; this idea will be developed further in the reflections on self-positing in fascicle VII. Toward the bottom of the same densely written page, Kant suggests that he wishes to identify "the real (of perception) in physics" and to "enumerate a priori these effects of the moving forces of the subject" (22:407). This is a very different formulation of the classificatory task previously ascribed to the elementary system: not the enumeration of the moving forces of matter, but the enumeration of the effects of the moving forces of the subject.

What Kant means by the "effects" of the subject's moving forces becomes clearer elsewhere in fascicles X/XI. The drafts show Kant thinking about forces, in the wider physiological sense, within the framework of action and reaction (*Wirkung und Gegenwirkung*). This is evidently a creative appropriation of the concepts contained in Newton's third law (cf. 4:545). Draft 'B' distinguishes four types of forces, only the first two of which are familiar from the *Metaphysical Foundations*: mechanical (through another body); dynamical (through an inner faculty for movement); organic (through an immaterial principle of inner purposiveness); and the force of will (*Willenskraft*). The latter is laconically glossed as "the moving forces, with consciousness, of humans" (22:307). Kant claims that these four types of force "contain all active relations of moving forces, which *physics* exerts on the object and to which the subject itself reacts" (22:308). As well as markedly expanding the scope of the forces belonging to physics, he here claims that physics (presumably meaning the physicist) exerts forces on objects, rather than simply researching the moving forces of these objects. Nevertheless, in this passage, the subject, although possessing moving forces "with consciousness," remains in the reactive position.

A significant shift on this point appears when Kant inverts the relation of activity and reactivity. Draft 'U' suggests: "The influence of the subject on the outer object and the reaction of the latter to the subject make it possible to cognize the moving forces of matter and so matter itself in substance, and to set them out for physics" (22:494). Without here referring to subjective forces specifically, Kant proposes that it is the influence of the subject on the object, rather than vice versa, that makes possible our knowledge of the forces of matter in physics. The subject is active, the object reactive.

Draft 'S' shows Kant wrestling with this idea. The folio begins straightforwardly enough by defining perception as "the mere relation of the object to the subject insofar as the latter is affected by the former." Here, the object affects the subject. However, Kant continues, "so an action <and reaction> of the moving forces, which the subject exerts on itself in apprehension <for the sake of sensation> <and to the subject objects are given as the materials of experience, which can always be nothing other than empirically affecting moving forces, even if the effects are also inner>" (22:453). The first two insertions, indicated by angle brackets, are added between the lines; the third is added in the top margin. They show that Kant initially describes only the action of the subject: the moving forces are those that "the subject exerts on itself in apprehension." What reacts to these moving forces of the subject are the objects given in experience, which are themselves, he adds, "empirically affecting moving forces."

Kant's most extensive explanation of this conception of the active and reactive moving forces of the subject and object, insofar as he provides one, can be found in draft 'X.' In the middle of the third page we read,

> The understanding has the faculty for making for itself an empirical representation from an object of the senses, and thereby also the perception of an object, even that it thereby stimulates [*erregt*] a priori the moving forces of the object on which it acts [*agirt*] to reciprocity [*wechselwirkung* (sic)]. – Now the understanding can enumerate a priori these actions with their reactions [*Actionen mit ihren Reactionen*], which only belong to perception, because they are mere relations of differing quality. (22:503)

Kant here claims that, through its faculty for empirically representing sense-objects, the understanding acts on the object and stimulates it to reciprocal activity. The actions and reactions, all of which are said to "belong to perception," should apparently be able to be enumerated. This enumeration differs once more from that of the elementary system: it now includes the actions of the understanding and the reactions of the object.

This idea, as speculative as it may sound, is further developed in a marginal note written next to the passage just quoted.

> The issue is as follows: perception is empirical representation with consciousness that it is such and not merely pure intuition of space. Now the effect [*Wirkung*] of the subject on the outer sense object represents this object in appearance, and indeed with the moving forces directed toward the subject, which are the cause of perception. So one can determine a priori those forces which effect [*bewirken*] perception as anticipations of sensible representation in empirical intuition, while one only presents (specifies) a priori the action and reaction [*Wirkung und Gegenwirkung*] of moving forces (under which belong, perhaps, understanding and desire), whose representation is identical to that of perception, according to principles of motion in general, which the understanding specifies and classifies as dynamic powers [*dynamische Potenzen*] according to the categories. (22:505)

Referring more generally to the subject rather than to the understanding, Kant reiterates the main text's idea that the object is stimulated to the reciprocal activity that causes perception. The subject acts upon the outer sense-object so that the latter directs its moving forces back at the subject. Not only the reactions of the object but also the actions of the subject are here described as "moving forces."

Two further notable ideas are introduced in this dense note. The first is that, as Kant tentatively suggests in parentheses, "perhaps, understanding and desire" should be numbered among the moving forces. An earlier passage, on page two of the folio, defines physics such that it encompasses "outer as well as inner empirical intuitions, as well as inner perceptions of the subject, i.e. sensations (called feelings if they contain pleasure or displeasure)" (22:500). Subjective sensations, and even feelings when accompanied with pleasure or displeasure, are here incorporated into a particularly broad conception of physics. A note on page four of the folio sums up the ideas Kant is exploring here: "Object of inner sense for sensation. To the moving forces also belongs human understanding. In the same, pleasure, displeasure and desire" (22:510). Remarkably, Kant is suggesting that the understanding, desire, and pleasure and displeasure, which the third *Critique* listed as the higher faculties examined by the critical philosophy (cf. 5:197–8, 20:346), should be conceived of as moving forces.

Second, Kant claims that his conception of the active moving forces of the subject and the counteracting moving forces of the object makes it possible to "determine a priori" the moving forces of the object and "anticipat[e] ... sensible representation in empirical intuition." This is another striking idea. Kant seems to suggest that the specific *given* content of sensibility can be determined in advance of experience. Borrowing a term from the first *Critique*, he calls this an anticipation. A passage on the same page develops this point:

> With regard to matter and those of its forces which <externally> affect the subject (hence are *moving* forces), perceptions themselves are in themselves moving forces combined with reaction (*reactio*), and the understanding *anticipates* perception according to the uniquely possible forms of motion – attraction, repulsion, enclosure (surrounding) and penetration. – Thus the possibility of establishing a priori a system of empirical representations (which otherwise appeared impossible) and of *anticipating* experience <*quoad materiale* [as material]> is illuminated (22:502).[68]

Kant here proposes four "forms of motion" through which perception can be anticipated: attraction and repulsion, which are familiar from the *Metaphysical Foundations*, and also "enclosure" and "penetration." This is an unusual quadripartite depiction of the forces of matter that does not appear elsewhere in the *Opus postumum*. More significant is Kant's claim that this makes possible the anticipation of experience *quoad materiale*. As we shall see in Section 5.8, this point is significant for many interpreters.

In this subsection we have considered Kant's investigation into the moving forces of the subject, which, he suggests, include the higher faculties of understanding, desire, and pleasure and displeasure. These forces should stimulate the object to reciprocity, causing it to direct its moving forces toward the subject and consequently cause perceptions. Kant claims that such a conception of the

---

[68] I have argued elsewhere that this note, which is written at the bottom of page three of the folio and continues a thought from the previous page, was the first thing to have been written on this page. It is unusual for Kant to write beyond the bounds of a page; I consider this to indicate the significance of this note for him (see Howard 2018: 78–9, and Appendix, section A.1).

interaction of subject and object should permit a complete enumeration of these actions and reactions, an enumeration that seems intended to fulfill the classificatory aims he had previously ascribed to the elementary system.

Although Kant's proposals here are undoubtedly strange and speculative, they may not be as far from basic positions of the critical philosophy as they appear at first sight. In the *Critiques*, the various activities of the mind are designated as forces (*Kräfte*) (see Heßbrüggen-Walter 2004: 126–67; Dyck 2014: 200–7).[69] What is new in fascicles X/XI of the *Opus postumum*, however, is that mental forces are depicted as *moving* and in direct interaction with physical forces. Kant's further step – that this conception allows the matter and not just the form of experience to be anticipated – will be addressed in Section 5.8. In any case, Kant is fully aware of the strangeness of the ideas that he is here exploring in his attempt to solve the transition problem. He repeatedly acknowledges that his proposals seem "disconcerting," "astounding," "paradoxical," "outright impossible."[70] But the strange new ideas allow him to achieve something that previously seemed impossible, as he puts it in 'S': "If, instead of matter (*Stoff*) I take moving forces of matter, and instead of the moveable object I take the moving subject, then what previously seemed impossible becomes possible, namely to represent empirical representations, which the subject itself makes according to the formal principle of connection a priori, as given" (22:455).

These two transpositions – for matter, the moving forces, and for the moveable object, the moving subject – give Kant a way to conceive of empirical representations as at once made a priori by the subject and yet given. This, I suggest, is the response to the transition problem that Kant is exploring in fascicles X/XI.

5.8 Anticipation *Quoad Materiale* or *Forma Dat Esse Rei?*

A debate in mid-twentieth-century *Opus postumum* scholarship can illuminate the ideas just sketched. We have seen Kant propose that the transition can and should anticipate the *material* element of experience, not just its formal

---

[69] Moreover, the passages we have considered are among those that Adickes (1920: 260–5) considers relevant for the debate over 'double affection' – an interpretative debate that pertains to the critical works as much as to the *Opus postumum* (see footnote 9 above, Hogan 2009, and Stang 2015). Lacking space to discuss this further, let me just suggest that Adickes' interpretation gets things the wrong way around. In my view, in fascicles X/XI Kant is not trying to clarify his doctrine of double affection; rather, he returns to the issue of affection because he believes it could help him solve the transition problem of securing the systematicity of physics.

[70] For references, see Mathieu 1989: 142. Kant already noted in the first *Critique*, however, that the Anticipations of Perception seemed disconcerting (*befremdlich*) and that there was something striking (*etwas Auffallendes*) in them for the researcher accustomed to the transcendental approach (A167/B209, A175/217). Little attention has been given to the relationship between the Anticipations and the transition project; an exception is Edwards 2004: 163–70.

element. This would be an anticipation of experience *quoad materiale*. Kant uses this phrase only a few times in the drafts.[71] Nevertheless, it is central to the interpretations of Adickes (1920: 163, 261–5); Lehmann (1969: 261, 280–4); Mathieu (1989: 141–4, cf. 128–31); and Edwards (2000: 153, 159). These commentators concur in viewing Kant's doctrine of material anticipation as a major novelty of the *Opus postumum*.

A strident rejection of this reading is offered by Hoppe. As he points out, the notion of an anticipation of the matter of experience seems to blatantly contradict the position of the first *Critique* (Hoppe 1969: 2). In the 1781/7 work, the *formal* structures of possible experience, that is, the forms of intuition and the categories of the understanding, can be known a priori, as can certain general laws, namely, the synthetic a priori propositions contained in the principles of the understanding. However, the specific *matter* or content of experience is only known a posteriori, and likewise the specific empirical laws of nature.

Hoppe therefore insists that the Latin phrase most relevant to the overall project of the *Opus postumum* is not anticipation *quoad materiale* but *forma dat esse rei*. The latter phrase, "form gives being (or essence) to a thing," is borrowed by Kant from the scholastics (see 21:641). He notes this provenance when he uses the phrase in "On A Superior Tone" (1796), the essay briefly discussed in Section 3.2. Schlosser and his band of mystical Platonists, the target of Kant's polemic, sneer at the practice of attending to the formal aspect of knowledge: they call this a pedantic "pattern-factory" (*Formgebungsmanufactur*). Kant counters that attention to form is "the preeminent business of philosophy." Here he cites the motto, *forma dat esse rei*, and adds, "insofar as the essence should be known through reason" (8:404, see Pollok 2017: 141–2). The implication, in the polemical context of the essay, is that considerations of the form of our knowledge instead of its matter keeps us to the secure path of transcendental critique, safe from the enthusiasm to which the mystical Platonists succumb.

In the *Opus postumum*, Kant often links *forma dat esse rei* to the claim that we cannot take anything from physics (or from experience) beyond what we insert into it (*hineinlegen*) (e.g. 22:306; for further passages, see Hoppe 1969: 116). This is a point that appears in the B Preface to the first *Critique* (Bxviii), concluding the famous discussion of Galilei, Torricelli, and Stahl, as Hoppe (1969: 115) points out. Hoppe insists that what Kant thinks must be inserted in the transition is the formal element of experience. As seen in Section 5.2, Hoppe ultimately argues that this formal insertion is intended to show how the experimental procedure of physics is possible (Hoppe 1969: 117). He considers

---

[71] 21:175, 22:345, 485, 502. Implicit allusions to the idea appear, for example, at 22:459, 504, 506.

fascicles X/XI the most important place in which this project unfolds: he points to the notions of the indirect object, or "appearance of the appearance," and the subject's self-affection, as key examples of formal elements that Kant claims should be inserted to this end (Hoppe 1969: 118–28).

On Hoppe's reading, the only time that Kant comes close to proposing that we can anticipate the *matter*, and not only the form, of experience is in the ether proofs: specifically, in Kant's attempts to prove that the ether constitutes a material principle of the unity of moving forces. Hoppe (1969: 111) claims that, for this reason, the ether proofs are only a way station for the development of ideas in the *Opus postumum*, one that Kant himself gives up. Kant abandons the attempt to prove the ether as a material principle of unity and proceeds to the more appropriate reflections in fascicles X/XI because the ether proofs "contradict Kant's fundamental axiom of the non-givenness of form" (Hoppe 1991: 61). His view of Kant's basic philosophical commitments leads Hoppe (1991: 56) to claim that even the third Analogy of the first *Critique* transgresses Kant's true position.[72]

Mathieu and Hoppe effectively conducted a slow-motion debate on this topic across more than three decades. In his 1969 book, Hoppe identified Mathieu's 1958 Italian study as the main recent representative of the view he wished to counter (Hoppe 1969: 1, 27–9, 110–14, 133–7). Mathieu responded to Hoppe in an excursus to the reworked 1989 German version of his Italian book (Mathieu 1989: 128–36). Hoppe fired the last salvo in the debate in his essay in the *Übergang* collection (Hoppe 1991). The debate essentially concerns whether we should take seriously Kant's suggestion that the transition project should anticipate experience *quoad materiale*: Mathieu says yes; Hoppe, as seen above, says no.

In response to Hoppe, Mathieu (1989: 134–6) rightly shows that Kant does not drop the ether proof in fascicles X/XI; rather, the existence of the ether is often assumed in the 1799–1800 drafts (see also Howard 2019: 611–12). In Mathieu's view, the *Übergang 1–14* drafts show "the metamorphosis of the ether into a transcendental principle," a transcendental condition that Kant takes in fascicles X/XI to be "undoubtedly *valid*" (Mathieu 1989: 123, 134). Regarding the possibility of the anticipation of the material element of experience, Mathieu (1989: 130) notes that Kant acknowledges that this task is "disconcerting" and "seems outright impossible." Kant is therefore conscious of the (at least potential) discrepancy between his new endeavor and the results reached in the first *Critique*. This novel character of the *Opus postumum*,

---

[72] The work of Edwards (1991, 2000) on the relation between the ether proofs and the third Analogy can be seen as an implicit counter to Hoppe's claim here.

Mathieu argues, is downplayed by Hoppe. As Mathieu (1989: 131) pointedly asks: if, as Hoppe claims, Kant intended only to express what he had already said in the *Critique*, why did he want to write a new work?

I propose that we can read the Mathieu–Hoppe debate as constituting an antinomy, according to certain aspects of Kant's sense of the term. Each side of an antinomy, Kant writes in the *Critique*, is strong when on the attack but unable to defend itself (A422–3/B450–1). Both Mathieu and Hoppe are convincing when they attack the other's position, but less so when trying to defend their own positive claims against the other. For example, Hoppe is wrong to suggest that Kant drops the concept of the ether and the necessity of its proof in fascicles X/XI, but Mathieu is wrong to claim that the ether has been unambiguously proved in the *Übergang 1–14* drafts as an apodictic transcendental principle. Hoppe can correctly argue that Kant refers to anticipation *quoad materiale* less often than he writes *forma dat esse rei*, but Mathieu can counter that Hoppe cannot deny that Kant nevertheless *does* refer to anticipation *quoad materiale*.[73]

This antinomy can be resolved in a manner similar to Kant's treatment of the antinomies in the first *Critique*. Mathieu and Hoppe, I would argue, are asking the wrong question. They are expecting Kant to take a single, unambiguous position on whether it is possible to anticipate the matter or only the mere form of experience. Both commentators here fail to read the late drafts as a work in progress. Kant is exploring *both* the view that what we insert into experience for the sake of the systematic unity of physics is merely formal *and* that we can anticipate the matter of experience. We could alternatively say that both Mathieu's and Hoppe's interpretations are correct from a certain perspective, namely, if one considers the drafts to be unfinished and inconclusive. Neither position represents Kant's fully articulated view – which he never reached – but only options that he was exploring.

5.9 Fascicles X/XI and Fascicle I: Understanding and Reason

We can consider one last aspect of the investigations into the concept of physics in fascicles X/XI: the notion of the world system. In a marginal note next to the four definitions of physics in draft 'A' that we examined in Section 5.3, Kant distinguishes between the formal and material senses of the "unity of experience as system of perceptions." We can set aside the formal unity, which stems from a "subjective principle," and focus instead on Kant's definition of the material unity of experience: "the idea of a whole of moving forces as the absolute (unconditioned) unity of the world system where the moving forces contain and initiate nothing outside their *complexus*" (22:300). The unity of experience in its

---

[73] On the latter point, see Basile 2013: 390.

material sense is here characterized as absolute or unconditioned and is equated with the world system.

Kant introduces the world system alongside the elementary system in the drafts of October 1798 to May 1799. He suggests that the two systems provide a division that structures the transition project:

> *First part*: the elementary system of the moving forces of matter
> *Second part*: the world system.[74]

This division is decisive for Mathieu's interpretation. He proposes to speculatively reconstruct Kant's projected work on the basis of these two parts (Mathieu 1989: 72–5, 79–83). According to Mathieu, the part of the manuscript on the elementary system, which includes the ether proofs, was left by Kant in a fairly finalized state, whereas the world system, said to contain topics treated in fascicles X, XI, VII, and I, remained fragmentary.

A different reading is provided by Emundts. In "Element. System 7," Kant states that "The elementary system is that which proceeds from the parts to the entire sum total of matter (without *hiatus*); the world system is that which proceeds from the idea of the whole to the parts" (22:200; cf. 22:197, 22:267). Borrowing a distinction from the *Inaugural Dissertation*, we can say that the elementary system follows the synthetic procedure while the world system follows the analytic procedure (2:387–8). On the same page of "Element. System 7," Kant adds that the elementary system is prior to the world system (22:201). Emundts (2004: 145–7) argues that, in the Elementary System drafts, the elementary system is logically prior to the world system, but the world system contains the real grounds of the elementary system, that is, it provides the notion of the ether as the absolute whole of matter. The elementary and the world systems would thus be different presentations of the same content, the totality of the moving forces of matter (Emundts 2004: 146).

Emundts' depiction of the relation between the elementary and world systems is convincing – if we restrict ourselves, as she does, to the drafts prior to August 1799. However, as argued in Sections 5.4 and 5.5, I consider Kant's conception of the place and status of the elementary system to change in fascicles X/XI. If this is correct, it means that the elementary system is no longer the first logical step in Kant's argument, as Emundts claims, nor does it form the first part of Kant's projected work, as Mathieu proposes. The classificatory elementary system plays an increasingly minor role in the transition

---

[74] 22:155. For related passages, see Mathieu 1989: 73. Caygill (2005: 34) points out that this plan for Kant's projected work recalls the structure of Newton's *Principia*, book 3 of which is titled "On the System of the World."

project as Kant conceives of it in 1799–1800; instead, the doctrinal system is central to Kant's intensive rethinking of the notion of physics.

Is there a corresponding shift in 1799–1800 in Kant's conception of the world system? And how does this relate to the "system of ideas" that Kant introduces in the final fascicles VII and I? While Kant often distinguishes between the elementary system and the doctrinal system in fascicles X/XI, he rarely differentiates the world system from the doctrinal system. Draft 'U' states that the world system is contained alongside the elementary system within the doctrinal system of natural science; the latter is equated with physics (22:487). The world system, "if it should represent an absolute whole, is a mere idea to which no object can therefore be adequately given, but which is nevertheless not a non-thing (*nonens*) but a thought-thing (*ens rationis*)" (22:485, see 22:300). Draft 'B' explicitly depicts the transition project in cosmological terms: the whole of perceptions is combined and connected under a principle into a world-whole (*Weltganze*) (22:308). Kant adds that "the whole [*All*] (το παν) of outer sense objects" constitutes the matter of the *Weltganze*, alongside the form provided by the system. His use of the Greek harks back to the definitions of the world in German metaphysics textbooks (see Baumgarten [1739] 2013: §354). Kant here defines the doctrinal system of physics as "only an *idea* of a science understood as never fully attainable but continually progressing, for which we have principles to research the elementary knowledge [*Elementarkentnissen*] but which we can never encapsulate in a completed system" (22:309–10, my emphasis). These passages present the doctrinal system of physics as either *containing* or *itself* the world system, where the latter is grounded on the mere idea of an absolute whole.

Even when Kant does not refer to the world system in fascicles X/XI, he consistently defines the doctrinal system of physics as concerned with the *whole* of perceptions or moving forces, that is, with experience or matter in the singular.[75] In this sense, as we have seen, the subjective doctrinal system can be complete even if its object, the objective elementary system, has a never-ending classificatory task. The doctrinal system should be able to be completed because it does not treat the objective *empirical whole of appearances*, the infinite variety of matter and its forces, but rather the subjective *whole of empirical appearances* (see 22:481–2). In this respect it corresponds to the world system, which progresses from the whole to the parts.

This said, there seems to be a fundamental difference between the prevailing conception of the doctrinal system in fascicles X/XI and the world system. Kant's references to the world system in fascicles X/XI anticipate the "system of

---

[75] See, for example, 22:299, 346, 360, 377, 402, 463, 509, 514.

ideas" in the final fascicle I: God, world, and man-in-the-world.[76] But the cognitive faculty to which Kant generally refers when discussing the doctrinal system is not reason but the understanding; not the *idea* of a unified experience or a unified matter, but their *concept*. Draft 'X' states, for example,

> It is not through compilation but according to a principle of connection of the moving forces of matter in a system that the moving forces of matter – that is, in relation to the possibility of the object for the sake of experience, empirical intuitions (perceptions) – can yield an a priori cognition of the object. The *understanding* is thus, subjectively, the principle of the possibility of making sense-objects into one experience as an aggregate of empirical representations. The axioms of pure intuition, as the principle of form, are followed by the anticipations of experience. (22:509)

Here, there is no need for an idea of reason to unify the system of perceptions and of moving forces; the understanding performs this function, through its system of principles. In fascicles X/XI, Kant regularly refers to the principles of the understanding, and particularly the Axioms and the Anticipations, as key to the task of physics in its newly expanded, physiological sense.[77] As draft 'T' states, "The transition consists, namely, in progressing, *by means of the under-standing*, from an aggregate of perceptions of oneself, to a system of percep-tions in one experience in general (that is, to physics as a doctrinal system)" (22:478, my emphasis). Kant here seeks to ground the systematicity of physics not on the mere idea of the whole, as will be the case in fascicle I, but on the principles of the understanding, insofar as they subjectively unify experience.

This should help show how Kant's turn in fascicle I to the "system of ideas" is a comprehensible development in the transition project. This development justifies neither the explicit 'two-work theory,' put forward in the late nineteenth century by Krause and Vaihinger, nor the implicit version of this theory arguably affirmed by recent interpreters who ignore the final fascicle. As I have argued, Kant's conception of physics widens in fascicles X/XI to encompass the totality of physical and psychological forces, the whole of matter and experience, and the actions and reactions of perceptions and material moving forces. Physics is not merely an infinitely progressing collection of observational and experimental data for which a distinct science of transition should provide a systematic basis. Rather, physics is *itself* systematic. In fascicles X/XI, the doctrinal system of physics contains the elementary system as its indefinite task, and it is difficult to distinguish it from the world system, in which the idea of the whole has precedence over the parts. However, while in fascicle I Kant will turn to reason's pure ideas, in fascicles

---

[76] For a discussion of the concept of world and the system of ideas in fascicle I, see Lehmann 1969: 263–70.

[77] See 22:281, 292–3, 300, 326, 338, 342, 366, 494, 504.

X/XI he is focused on the role of the understanding and its principles, particularly the Axioms and the Anticipations. Fascicles X/XI and fascicle I therefore take two perspectives, those of the understanding and of reason, on the problem of the systematic unification of the moving forces of matter and the subject's perceptions.

6 Conclusion

We have seen that a sharp objection to the basic aim of Kant's project in the *Opus postumum* was raised by Adickes and Tuschling (Section 5.2). On their view, Kant's attempt to systematize empirical physics a priori was fundamentally misguided, and the transition project was always destined to lead to failure. This is because physics is properly defined not by its systematicity but by its method of observation and experiment. Systematic unity is not a criterion that precedes physics but only a "strived-for but never-attained aim at its end" (Adickes 1920: 362). Hoppe agrees with this characterization of physics, but he attempts to salvage the *Opus postumum* by arguing that Kant intends to present there only the formal a priori conditions of physics. But this would mean, as Mathieu points out, that Kant's claims in the late drafts are at heart indistinguishable from those in the first *Critique* – which cannot explain why Kant went to such great lengths to try to write a new work (Section 5.8).

When Adickes, Tuschling, and Hoppe claim that physics is properly characterized by its observational and experimental method and that systematicity is merely a dispensable supplement, they ignore Kant's intensive engagement in fascicles X/XI with the very question of how physics might be conceived of as a system. Can the natural philosopher only anticipate the mere *form* of empirical physics through the categories and transcendental laws already provided by the first *Critique*? Or is it possible to anticipate the *matter* of physics, that is, its specific empirical results regarding the moving forces of bodies? These two poles are associated in the drafts with the Latin mottos, *forma dat esse rei* and anticipation *quoad materiale*. I have argued that the interpretations of Hoppe and Mathieu, which insist on the centrality of the former and the latter respectively, produce an antinomy (Section 5.8). This is because the two commentators fail to appreciate that Kant is exploring where to locate himself between these extremes.[78] That is, he seeks to precisely determine which elements of physics

---

[78] Edwards (2000: 138, 159, 242 n.44, 2004: 159–60, 175, 187) has an overall interpretation comparable to mine: he argues that in the transition project we see a "collapse" of Kant's critical distinction between the a priori and the empirical levels of our knowledge of nature. I agree that this distinction is the central problem at stake in Kant's late project. However, I place more emphasis on the unfinished character of the drafts: rather than definitively undermining the a priori–empirical distinction, I consider Kant to be exploring different approaches to the problem of bridging the a priori and empirical elements of physics.

are fixed and can be determined a priori, and which change in line with developments in our empirical knowledge.

Stepping back from the *Opus postumum* literature, we can see that the problem with which Kant was grappling bears striking similarities with certain concerns of late neo-Kantian and early logical empiricist philosophers. In the wake of the establishment of non-Euclidean mathematics and Einstein's theories of relativity, these thinkers were troubled by whether Kant's a priori conditions of possible experience, viewed as attempts to secure Newtonian physics in particular, remained tenable.[79] Were not the Kantian pure forms of intuition and principles discredited by these developments in physics? The issue famously spurred Hans Reichenbach, who studied with Ernst Cassirer in Berlin, to develop the notion of the 'constitutive a priori.' Reichenbach claimed that this sense of the a priori referred not to eternal and unchanging conditions but to a framework that constitutes the object of scientific knowledge.[80] As Michael Friedman (2001: 30–1) has emphasized, Reichenbach thus presents a "relativized" or "dynamical" conception of the a priori, according to which the constitutive conditions of knowledge are partly empirical and can be revised in the light of new scientific developments.[81]

Of course, Kant had no inkling of the revolutionary upheavals that would transform mathematics and physics from the mid-nineteenth to the early twentieth century. Nevertheless, on my reading of the *Opus postumum*, he was concerned with the same general issue as his later followers and critics: namely, whether empirical physics, despite its indefinite and unforeseeable progress, contains elements that can be determined a priori. But Kant does not take Reichenbach's step of revising the transcendental conditions that are set out in the first *Critique*. There is no hint in the *Opus postumum* that the categories of substance, cause, and so on, are not still the basic concepts of objects in general, nor that the synthetic a priori principles based on them, such as the law of causality, become invalid.[82] Kant's investigation in the *Opus postumum*

---

[79] For some classic statements, see Schlick [1915] 2019; Reichenbach [1920] 1965: 1–33, 61–73; and Cassirer [1921] 1923: 352–5.

[80] Reichenbach [1920] 1965: 48–60. 'Framework' is here shorthand for what Reichenbach ([1920] 1965: 60) calls "a system of coordinating principles."

[81] Reichenbach's position is further developed by Carnap (see Friedman 2001: 31–3) and by Friedman himself (see Friedman 2001: 71–92). Watkins (2019: 41–6) insists on the distance between Carnap's views and Kant's own.

[82] Some readers have taken Kant to newly ascribe transcendental status to the ether in the proofs attempted in May to August 1799 (see particularly Edwards 2000 and Rollman 2015). Regardless of the debates over this view (see Howard 2019: 600–5), we can note that even this reading takes Kant to at most *supplement* the categories and principles of the understanding with an additional material transcendental condition, not to revise the existing transcendental conditions.

proceeds on a different level: it explores the boundary between the a priori and empirical elements *specific to physics*. It is on this level that Kant experiments with different intermediary concepts and, in fascicles X/XI, different conceptions of physics.

Debates will no doubt continue to rage over the extent of the continuities and discontinuities between the canonical works of 1781–90 and the *Opus postumum*. In this Element, I have argued that these debates can best be approached not from the perspective of the 'gap' that Kant is seeking to fill in his previous philosophy, but from the perspective of the new transition project and the question of the systematicity of physics. Now, let me add in closing that there is one aspect of Kant's position in the first *Critique* that unquestionably remains at the heart of his late reflections, but which has been widely neglected by *Opus postumum* scholars. This is Kant's conception of reason. The faculty, in its theoretical use, continually seeks the totality of conditions: it strives for complete explanation. Kant depicts this through the famous image of the "peculiar fate" of reason, with which the first *Critique* begins, and by claiming that reason has a "natural propensity" to overstep its boundaries, boundaries that the critical philosophy seeks to determine.[83]

The early drafts of the *Opus postumum* contain regular references to the "natural tendency" of the metaphysical foundations toward physics.[84] Kant glosses this tendency toward physics as a "natural ostension [*Hinweisung*] of reason to an end" (22:166, cf. 21:289). As we saw in Section 3, the earliest drafts of the transition project were contemporaneous with Kant's reflections on progressing from the sensible to the supersensible. This is a very different (even, I suggested, the opposite) transition to the one usually at stake in the *Opus postumum*. Nevertheless, in both cases a boundary is identified, whether between the sensible and the supersensible or between metaphysical foundations and physics, which human reason cannot help transgressing. The question, for Kant, is not whether this happens – because it is inevitable – but rather how such an overstepping can be conducted legitimately.

Kant's death meant that his explorations were inconclusive – if indeed such an ambitious project could ever be definitively completed. This may be unsatisfying for many readers. But we cannot pretend that the *Opus postumum* is other than it is: Kant's unfinished late attempt to address the transition problem. The drafts remain a remarkable record of his efforts and the shifts in his thinking on the topic. Kant's final project implies that, as rational beings, we cannot help but try to systematize physics. Anyone who would quickly dismiss this as an

---

[83] Avii, A642/B670. On Kant's conception of reason, see Willaschek 2018: 6, 22–3. On the critical project of boundary-determination, see Howard 2022.

[84] See, all from the Elementary System drafts: 21:289, 528, 616, 617, 621, 630, 636, 22:164, 166.

outdated ambition should consider the range of figures in the history of physics with 'unifying' ambitions.[85] Kant's own sustained and creative attempt to construct a bridge between metaphysics and the specific results of physics cannot be subsumed into the neo-Kantian or logical empiricist attempts at the same task. For just this reason, the *Opus postumum* is worthy of our continued attention.

---

[85] Hacking (1996) sketches a history of conceptions of unity and disunity in the sciences with particular attention to 'unifiers' like James Clerk Maxwell.

Appendix
How to Read the Opus postumum

A.1 Kant's Writing Process

The *Opus postumum* presents unusual difficulties to the reader. When reading most works, it can be taken for granted that one begins at the top of a page and reads downwards, and one proceeds from the start of the book to the end. Not so with any edition of Kant's late drafts. The text is a record of Kant's thought processes as he attempted to develop a work. To be able to read it, we need to know how he wrote it, and more generally how his writing – the activity of making marks with a quill and ink on paper – relates to his published works.

Publication in the form of a work was of course the unrealized aim of the late drafts. Kant writes prefaces and introductions to a whole that did not (and still does not) exist. Because the process of finishing the work was interrupted by Kant's death (and may, in any case, have been rendered unattainable by the subject matter), no edition of the *Opus postumum* could ever reflect or approximate what Kant, had he lived longer, may have intended or gone on to produce. Any published version of Kant's *Opus postumum* is, strictly speaking, neither Kant's nor an *opus*. Instead, the text, however we access it, provides a fascinating insight into how one of the great figures in the history of Western philosophy thought, as Adickes (1897a: 53) remarks, "with his pen in his hand."

The *Opus postumum* drafts are notoriously repetitive: Kant makes innumerable attempts at the same passages, searching not just for better phrases but for solutions to the philosophical problems at hand. They thus shed light on his working method. Already in the *Philippi Logik* notes of 1772, Kant recommends to his students the following approach to philosophical "meditation":

> At the beginning one meditates tumultuously. One must write out that which comes to mind, if an occasional thought comes to mind that one has never had in one's life. First, one jots down all thoughts, as one has them, without order. After that, one begins to coordinate and then to subordinate. If one wants to produce something, one must certainly complete the skeleton of the system in general, and subsequently divide this into chapters. Thus every elaboration [*Außarbeitung*] must proceed with three tasks [*Arbeiten*]:

1. One jots down all thoughts, without order.
2. One makes a general plan.
3. One elaborates [*arbeitet . . . aus*] all the parts. (24:484)[86]

In this three-fold methodology, the process of "coordination and subordination" apparently facilitates the second stage's creation of the plan from the stream-of-consciousness notes produced in the first stage. As Adickes (1897b: 240) puts it, Kant "does not first conceptualize everything, content as much as presentation, finished in his head, but determines at most the train of thought in advance, then thinks through the particulars with his pen in his hand" (see Karl 2007: 127).

There is good reason to think that Kant worked like this throughout his long career. Borowski provides a similar account of his friend's writing method and adds that, in a final stage, Kant would rework the whole and copy it out for the printer (Borowski [1804] 2012: 78). At least by the late 1790s, Kant delegated this last step to an amanuensis. His student Kiesewetter, for example, wrote up much of the manuscript of the third *Critique* and later corrected the proofs. The *Opus postumum* contains evidence of this stage: there is an amanuensis' copy of the *Übergang 9, 10,* and *11* drafts, which Kant has heavily edited, crossing through much of it (22:543–55). Elsewhere, he notes down the amanuensis he would like to transcribe the text (21:44, 72).

Jacqueline Karl, who leads the transcription of the new Academy edition of the *Opus postumum* at the Berlin-Brandenburgische Akademie der Wissenschaften (BBAW), has outlined the principles of the "long overlooked, genetically oriented structural analysis" that underpins the new edition (Karl 2007: 134). This analysis highlights three steps in the composition of the *Opus postumum* manuscript. Kant's first step is to write the "main text" (which Karl calls the *Grundtext* and Lehmann the *Hauptteil*) in the middle of the page, with large margins left around the edges. In the second step, Kant corrects and stylistically alters the text between the lines and in marginal notes linked to the main text by vertical marks. The third step is to add marginal notes that more substantively rework the content of the main text. Kant links notes that run on from one another with symbols. This lets us see that the notes in this third step usually begin, chronologically, at the bottom of the page and progress from there around the side to the top of the page (Karl 2007: 130–1, 137–40; cf. Lehmann's introduction, 22:781–5). Karl (2007: 132) identifies various kinds of marginal note in this third step: "a progression or supplementation of the main text, a replacement, an alternative, a completed remark to the main text,

---

[86] Förster quotes two lines of this passage in Kant 1993: xxiv. See also 24:293. The recommended approach seems to be Kant's own; it is not in his textbook, Meier's *Vernunftlehre*: compare 16:811–13.

or an independent reflection." The BBAW online edition of the *Opus postumum* distinguishes the three steps of Kant's writing process (see section C).

Bringing together Karl's reconstruction with Kant's description in the *Philippi Logik* notes, we can identify all three stages described in the 1772 lectures in Kant's final drafts. That is, we often find that within a folio, or even on a single page, Kant writes stream-of-consciousness notes, subordinates and coordinates these thoughts into a general plan, and fleshes out this plan into a more finished philosophical text.

A helpful image for understanding Kant's writing process, to which Karl (2007: 134) also refers, is provided by Mathieu when he describes the manuscript as "cell-like." Kant wrote most of the *Opus postumum* on large sheets of paper folded once to make folios of four pages. Mathieu (1989: 61–3) points out that Kant almost never extended a thought beyond the bounds of a folio, nor even beyond a page; if he ran out of space, his writing got smaller and smaller, as was usually the case on the fourth page of a folio. This means that

> In principle, the unity of the thought corresponds to the pre-given formal unity of the paper (a page, a folio). In this respect the pages become at once *images of a train of thought*. The single sheet, often also the single page, has the task of incorporating the conclusive train of thought, and so attains a synoptic function. (Mathieu 1989: 62)

The synoptic function of each page and each folio is compared by Mathieu (1989: 62) to the cell of an organism, which contains the DNA of the whole body.

It is not a coincidence that Mathieu was a scholar of Leibniz as well as of Kant. He depicts the pages of Kant's manuscript as like monads, each mirroring the whole although from their various points of view, that is, from a particular stage of the development of Kant's thinking (Mathieu 1989: 63). Basile (2013: 362–3) rightly notes that Mathieu's appealing image cannot be taken too literally, as it would imply that the whole of the *Opus postumum* could be reconstructed from a single page. This is clearly not the case, particularly as Kant's thinking develops as the drafts progress, and indeed it develops *because of* this writing process. The early leaves therefore cannot already contain the positions that Kant will later develop "with his pen in his hand." In this Element I have stressed how Kant's thinking changed as he worked on the project. Mathieu's overly systematizing interpretation does not sufficiently attend to this developmental character. This is evident in his belief that he could reconstruct how Kant's final work would have been organized (Mathieu 1989: 79–83, see Section 5.9).

However, Mathieu's methodological proposal to read the drafts as cell-like or monadological should not be dismissed too quickly. Leibnizian monads are of course limited by the perspectives they occupy. While they mirror the entire universe, they represent only a part of it clearly, and most of their representations are obscure. The same could be said of the pages of Kant's manuscript: the early leaves may mirror the whole, but with near-total obscurity with regard to many of the later developments; such developments may only appear in a single word, which Kant will later take up and investigate in much more detail (for example, 'physics' or 'experience'). The way that individual pages mirror the whole can only be grasped from a 'God-like' perspective, to borrow the monadological terminology: from the perspective – which for us is unattainable – of a reader who knows what the final work would have looked like.

Although it may seem fanciful, Mathieu's proposal can have practical applications. Above, I sought to explain elements of the *Opus postumum* by expanding on compressed presentations in single passages. In Section 3, I explicated Kant's abstract conception of the transition on the basis of the first passage in which he discusses it. In Section 5, my analysis of Kant's shifting conceptions of physics developed out of the definitions in draft 'A,' where they can be seen *in nuce*. In both cases, I sought to clarify the 'obscure representations' of these compressed 'monadological' passages by referring to other pages where Kant takes up the same issues in more detail. My methodological proposal is therefore that, by taking seriously this cell-like character of the manuscript, we can attempt to combine the systematic ambitions of early twentieth-century interpretations with the rigour of the major studies published in the last fifty years. That is, we can combine close textual and historical analysis with claims about the overall project of the late drafts.

A.2 Phases and Dates

Table 1 gives the chronological order of the pages of the existing Buchenau–Lehmann Academy edition (AA) as well as of the fascicles and pages of the manuscript according to the new numbering system established by Tilo Brandis. The table is *not* a concordance between the AA pagination and the new numbering system; this would take up too much space. The third and fourth columns are therefore not correlated with each other, but are separate, chronologically ordered lists. A full concordance is provided by Brandis (in Kant 1999: 35–58).

The table combines the following: Brandis' chronological overview (Kant 1999: 35–60); Adickes' table of dates, included at the end of volume 22 of AA, which remains the basis of Brandis' dating; and the amendments by Tuschling (1971: 6–7). I have incorporated two corrections to Brandis' table from the version on the BBAW website.

I have split the drafts into five phases, with designations that are commonly used in the literature in the second column; in my view, this is a useful division

Table 1 Phases and dates of the manuscript

Estimated date	Draft name	AA volume and page no.	Fascicle and page no.
1786–96	Preparatory work and *Oktaventwurf*	21:415–73[1] 21:373–412	IV 41–84 XIII 1–4 IV 85–94 IV 13–40
July 1797– May 1799	Elementary system	21:307–34	III 25–36
		22:205–15	IX 5–8
		21:247–64	II 45–52
		21:495–504	V 5–8
		21:521–8[2]	V 17–20
		21:337–51	IV 1–4
		21:474–88	III 5–16
		21:174–81	II 11–14
		21:267–94	IV 97–102
		21:161–74	IV 95–6[3]
		21:352–61	IV 103–4
		22:246–67	II 5–10
		22:216–26	IV 5–8
		21:361–9	IX 21–8
		21:528–35	IX 9–12
		21:294–307	IV 9–12[4]
		21:504–12	V 21–4
		22:135–201	III 17–24
		21:615–45	V 9–12
		22:226–46	VIII 5–34
		21:181–206	VI 5–20
		22:267–76	IX 13–20
		22:585–609	II 15–24 IX 29–32 XII 29–40
May 1799– August 1799	Ether proofs	21:206–47	II 25–44
		21:535–612	V 25–60
		21:512–20	V 13–16
		22:609–15	XII 41–2
		22:556–85	XII 5–16
		21:488–92	XII 17–28 IV 105–8[5]
August 1799– April 1800	Fascicles X/XI	22:295–409	X 5–58
		22:453–539	XI 5–36
		22:425–52	

Table 1 (cont.)

Estimated date	Draft name	AA volume and page no.	Fascicle and page no.
April 1800– February 1803	Fascicles VII/I	22:3–31 22:409–21 21:9–158 21:3–9	VII 5–20 VII 27–46 X 59–62[6] I 1–48 VII 21–6

Notes

1 I agree with Tuschling and Förster that loose leaf 6 (21:474–7, IV 95–6) should be dated to August to September 1798 alongside leaves 3/4, 5, and 7: see footnote 14 above. Tuschling does not update the Academy edition pagination in the first entry of his table to take this change into account. Brandis does not alter Adickes' dating of loose leaf 6.

2 Missing in Adickes' table, added by Tuschling.

3 Loose leaf 6 inserted between 5 and 7.

4 Brandis' table corrected following https://kant.bbaw.de/de/abt-iii/faksimiles-op, accessed September 23, 2022.

5 Brandis' table corrected following https://kant.bbaw.de/de/abt-iii/faksimiles-op, accessed September 23, 2022.

6 It is widely recognized that this folio was misplaced in fascicle X and belongs in fascicle VII. See Adickes 1920: 143; Mathieu 1989: 250–1; Kant 1993: 179–85.

of the drafts. The designations are a mixture of descriptions of the content (e.g. "ether proofs"), names of the fascicles in which the drafts were bundled (e.g. "X/XI"), and, in one case, an allusion to the type of paper on which they were written ("*Oktaventwurf*," Adickes' term). More detailed designations, including Kant's own (such as "α–ε," "Farrago 1–4," "AB Übergang," etc.), and their estimated dates, can be found in Adickes' table, Tuschling (1971: 6–7), Kant (1999: 59–60), and Basile (2013: 502).

Throughout this Element, I have assumed that the dating is accurate and so have not repeatedly noted that the date is an approximation by Adickes or someone else. There is, of course, some uncertainty, although the general order and many of the specifics established by Adickes are generally accepted. On the dating, see Adickes (1920: 36–154), Förster (Kant 1993: xxvi–xxix), and Stark (1993: 140–51).

A.3 Editions of the *Opus postumum*

For any reader of the present Element, the best place to begin reading the *Opus postumum* is Eckart Förster's Cambridge edition. Its well-chosen selection provides an overview of all the phases of the drafts. If a passage has been highlighted in one of the classic interpretations, it is likely to be found translated by Förster and Rosen in this edition. The advantage of the Cambridge edition is that it is chronologically ordered, so even a reader of German may find it more helpful than the existing Academy edition as an entry point into the problems at stake in the drafts. The drafts are also chronologically ordered in the part-translations into Italian by Mathieu (Kant 1963), Spanish by Duque Pajuelo (Kant 1983), and French by Marty (Kant 1986), although not in Gibelin's earlier French translation (Kant 1950). Förster divides the text into seven phases: these are the same divisions that I make here but with what I call "fascicles VII/I" subdivided into three. The Cambridge edition contains a generous selection of passages from fascicles X/XI, which I have argued are particularly important (Förster gives them the title, "How is physics possible? How is the transition to physics possible?"). For further discussion of translations and references to other editions, see Basile (2013: 485–7, 506–7).

The 1936–8 Academy edition of the *Opus postumum* is notoriously flawed (see Basile 2013: 484–5). The main difficulty is Buchenau and Lehmann's "diplomatic" presentation of the drafts, which does not follow the chronological order already established by Adickes but reproduces the pages as they were found in the fascicles. As Helbig (2020: 67) puts it, "this diplomatic edition sanctified in print the random order imposed on the manuscript during its journeys" (see also Brandt 1991: 14). This means that the reader opening the Academy edition is first faced by fascicle I, which Kant wrote last. As can be seen from Table 1, a reader attempting to read the Elementary System drafts in their chronological order has an extremely complicated task of moving between disparate parts of both volumes of the Academy edition.

At the time of writing, Buchenau and Lehmann's edition is the fullest available in print. However, a new Academy edition is currently being prepared by the BBAW. Directed by Förster and Karl, this edition is accompanied by an online edition in which the raw transcriptions can be viewed next to the facsimiles of Kant's manuscript pages (Kant 2020). The online edition, now complete, is a fabulous resource. The facsimile and the transcription can be viewed side by side. The three phases of Kant's writing process (see section A.1 of this Appendix) are distinguished from each other. When one clicks on the facsimile, text from the first phase of Kant's writing is contained in a blue box, text from the second phase is in a red box, and that from the third phase in either green or, for "functional" rather than chronological variants, light blue boxes.

The BBAW online edition is invaluable for close work on individual pages of the manuscript. The transcription supersedes the readings in Buchenau and

Lehmann's edition. It is not an edition that one can really *read*, however.[87] For this, one must still turn to the more pragmatic 1936–8 edition, which Buchenau conceived so that "also the non-philologist has the courage . . . to really *use* it."[88] It remains to be seen how the new print edition of the Academy edition volumes 21–22 will seek to balance precision of transcription with readability, and how it will present the manuscript's main text, marginal notes, signs, deletions, corrections, and alterations on the printed page.

A final useful source is the Bonner Kant-Korpus (Kant 2007), an online reproduction of volumes 1–23 of the Academy edition. The digitized *Opus postumum* volumes include links to the facsimiles of each page of the manuscript in a more accessible way than the scans in the BBAW's online edition; these allow the reader to make their own attempt at deciphering Kant's handwriting.

---

[87] Helbig (2020) argues that the new digital edition has the effect of undermining the "monumentalization" of Kant's writings effected by the Academy edition since it was initiated by Dilthey because the drafts appear in the digital edition as neither a work nor a text but as an unruly constellation. Helbig also gives an insightful account of the variable effects of "piety" in the editing of the works of a great national philosopher.

[88] Letter from Buchenau to Adickes, May 27, 1925, quoted in Stark (1993: 109–10) and in Basile (2013: 481–2).

References

References to Kant's works are to the volume and page number of the Academy edition, Kant (1902–), except in the case of the *Critique of Pure Reason*, which is cited according to the A/B edition pagination. Volumes 21–22 of the Academy edition contain the *Opus postumum*. All translations of Kant's works are mine. I have compared my translations of the *Opus postumum* with the Cambridge edition (Kant 1993) when passages are contained therein. Kant's later insertions and marginal additions are signaled with angle brackets and his deletions with struck-through text.

Kant

Kant, Immanuel (1902–). *Kants Gesammelte Schriften*. Ed. Königlich Preußischen Akademie der Wissenschaften, later the Deutschen Akademie der Wissenschaften zu Berlin. Berlin: de Gruyter (and predecessors).

(1950). *Opus postumum. Textes choisis et traduits*. Ed. and (French) trans. Jean Gibelin. Paris: Vrin.

(1963). *Opus postumum*. Ed. and (Italian) trans. Vittorio Mathieu. Bologna: Zanichelli.

(1983). *Transición de los Principios metafísicos de la ciencia natural a la física (Opus postumum)*. Ed. and (Spanish) trans. Félix Duque Pajuelo. Madrid: Editora Nacional.

(1986). *Opus postumum. Passage des principes métaphysiques de la science de la nature à la physique*. Ed. and (French) trans. François Marty. Paris: PUF.

(1993). *Opus postumum*. Ed. Eckart Förster, (English) trans. Eckart Förster and Michael Rosen. Cambridge: Cambridge University Press.

(1999). *Opus postumum. Mikroficheausgabe*. Ed. Tilo Brandis. Berlin: Staatsbibliothek zu Berlin Preußischer Kulturbesitz.

(2007) *Das Bonner Kant-Korpus*. https://korpora.zim.uni-duisburg-essen.de/Kant/verzeichnisse-gesamt.html, accessed September 23, 2022.

(2020) *Opus postumum Online-Edition*. Berlin-Brandenburgische Akademie der Wissenschaften. http://telota.bbaw.de/kant_op/index.html, accessed September 23, 2022.

Secondary and Other Sources

Adickes, Erich (1897a). "Die bewegenden Kräfte in Kants philosophischer Entwicklung und die beiden Pole seines Systems." *Kant-Studien* 1: 9–59, 161–96, 352–415.

(1897b). "Lose Blätter aus Kants Nachlass." *Kant-Studien* 1: 232–300.

(1920). *Kants Opus postumum. Dargestellt und beurteilt.* Berlin: Reuther und Reichard.

(1922). "Zur Lehre von der Wärme von Fr. Bacon bis Kant." *Kant-Studien* 27: 328–68.

(1924–5). *Kant als Naturforscher.* 2 vols. Berlin: de Gruyter.

(1929). *Kants Lehre von der Doppelten Affektion unseres Ich als Schlüssel zu seiner Erkenntnistheorie.* Tübingen: Mohr.

Basile, Giovanni Pietro (2013). *Kants Opus postumum und seine Rezeption.* Berlin: de Gruyter.

(2019). "The Doctrine of Double Affection in the Earlier Reception of Kant's *Opus postumum*" in Violetta L. Waibel, Margit Ruffing, and David Wagner eds., *Natur und Freiheit. Akten des XII. Internationalen Kant-Kongresses.* Berlin: de Gruyter, 3639–47.

Baumgarten, Alexander [1739] (2013). *Metaphysics.* Ed. and trans. Courtney D. Fugate and John Hymers. London: Bloomsbury.

Beiser, Frederick C. (2002). *German Idealism: The Struggle against Subjectivism 1781–1801.* Cambridge, MA: Harvard University Press.

Blasche, Siegfried, Wolfgang Köhler, Wolfgang Kuhlmann, and Peter Rohs. Eds. (1991). *Übergang. Untersuchungen zum Spätwerk Immanuel Kants.* Frankfurt: Vittorio Klostermann.

Blomme, Henny (2015). "La notion de 'système' chez Wolff, Lambert et Kant." *Estudos Kantianos* 3.1: 105–26.

Borowski, Ludwig Ernst [1804] (2012). *Darstellung des Lebens und Charakters Immanuel Kants* in *Immanuel Kant. Sein Leben in Darstellungen von Zeitgenossen.* Darmstadt: WBG.

Brandt, Reinhard (1991). "Kants Vorarbeiten zum Übergang von der Metaphysik der Natur zur Physik. Probleme der Edition" in Blasche, Köhler, Kuhlmann, and Rohs eds., 1–27.

Breitenbach, Angela (2018). "Laws and Ideal Unity" in Walter Ott and Lydia Patton eds., *Laws of Nature.* Oxford: Oxford University Press, 108–22.

Cassirer, Ernst [1921] (1923). *Einstein's Theory of Relativity* in *Substance and Function and Einstein's Theory of Relativity.* Trans. William Curtis Swabey and Marie Collins Swabey. Chicago, IL: Open Court.

Caygill, Howard (2005). "The Force of Kant's *Opus postumum*: Kepler and Newton in the XIth Fascicle." *Angelaki* 10: 33–42.

de Vleeschauwer, Herman J. (1937). *La Déduction Transcendantale dans l'œuvre de Kant. Tome III: La Déduction Transcendantale de 1787 Jusqu'à l'Opus postumum*. Antwerp: De Sikkel.

Dyck, Corey (2014). *Kant and Rational Psychology*. Oxford: Oxford University Press.

Edwards, Jeffrey (1991). "Der Ätherbeweis des Opus postumum und Kants 3. Analogie der Erfahrung" in Blasche, Köhler, Kuhlmann, and Rohs eds., 77–104.

(2000). *Substance, Force, and the Possibility of Knowledge: On Kant's Philosophy of Nature*. Berkeley: University of California Press.

(2004). "One More Time: Kant's Metaphysics of Nature and the Idea of Transition" in Cinzia Ferrini ed., *Eredità kantiane (1804–2004). Questioni emergenti e problemi irrisolti*. Naples: Bibliopolis, 155–88.

(2008). "'Transition' and 'Gap' in Kant's *Opus postumum*" in Valerio Rohden, Ricardo R. Terra, Guido A. de Almeida, and Margit Ruffing eds., *Akten des 10. internationalen Kant-Kongresses* vol. 5. Berlin: de Gruyter, 231–43.

Emundts, Dina (2004). *Kants Übergangskonzeption im Opus postumum*. Berlin: de Gruyter.

Engelhard, Kristina (2018). "The Problem of Grounding Natural Modality in Kant's Account of Empirical Laws of Nature." *Studies in History and Philosophy of Science* 71: 24–34.

Förster, Eckart (1987). "Is There 'a Gap' in Kant's Critical System?" *Journal of the History of Philosophy* 25.4: 533–55.

(2000). *Kant's Final Synthesis: An Essay on the Opus postumum*. Cambridge, MA: Harvard University Press.

(2003). "Reply to Friedman and Guyer." *Inquiry* 46.2: 228–38.

Friedman, Michael (1992). *Kant and the Exact Sciences*. Cambridge, MA: Harvard University Press.

(2001). *Dynamics of Reason*. Stanford, CA: CSLI Publications.

(2003). "Eckart Förster and Kant's *Opus postumum*." *Inquiry* 46.2: 215–27.

Gloy, Karen (1976). *Die Kantische Theorie der Naturwissenschaft. Eine Strukturanalyse ihrer Möglichkeit, ihres Umfangs und ihrer Grenzen*. Berlin: de Gruyter.

Hacking, Ian (1996). "The Disunities of the Sciences" in Peter Galison and David Stump eds., *The Disunity of Science*. Stanford, CA: Stanford University Press, 37–74.

Hall, Bryan Wesley (2015). *The Post-Critical Kant: Understanding the Critical Philosophy through the Opus Postumum*. London: Routledge.

Helbig, Daniela K. (2020). "Gebäude auf Abbruch? The Digital Archive of Kant's *Opus postumum.*" *Aisthesis* 13.2: 59–77.

Heßbrüggen-Walter, Stefan (2004). *Die Seele und ihre Vermögen: Kants Metaphysik des Mentalen in der Kritik der reinen Vernunft.* Paderborn: Mentis.

Hogan, Desmond (2009). "Noumenal Affection." *Philosophical Review* 118.4: 501–32.

Hoppe, Hansgeorg (1969). *Kants Theorie der Physik. Eine Untersuchung über das Opus postumum von Kant.* Frankfurt: Klostermann.

(1991). "Forma dat esse rei. Inwiefern heben wir in der Erkenntnis das aus der Erfahrung nur heraus, was wir zuvor in sie hineingelegt haben?" in Blasche, Köhler, Kuhlmann, and Rohs eds., 49–64.

Howard, Stephen (2018). "The Material Literary Form of Kant's *Opus postumum.*" *Pli: The Warwick Journal of Philosophy* 29: 65–87.

(2019). "The Transition within the Transition: the *Übergang* from the *Selbstsetzungslehre* to the Ether Proofs in Kant's *Opus postumum.*" *Kant-Studien* 110.4: 595–617.

(2022). "Kant on Limits, Boundaries, and the Positive Function of Ideas." *European Journal of Philosophy* 30: 64–78.

(2023). "Physics as System in Fascicles X/XI" in Giovanni Pietro Basile and Ansgar Lyssy eds., *Perspectives on Kant's Opus postumum.* London: Routledge.

Kain, Patrick (2010). "Practical Cognition, Intuition, and the Fact of Reason" in James Krueger and Benjamin J. Bruxvoort Lipscomb eds., *Kant's Moral Metaphysics.* Berlin: de Gruyter, 211–30.

Karl, Jacqueline (2007). "Immanuel Kant – der Autor, der 'mit der Feder in der Hand' denkt: Die Arbeitsweise Kants als ein Kriterium für die Neuedition des *Opus postumum*" in Annette Sell ed., *Editionen – Wandel und Wirkung.* Tübingen: Max Niemeyer Verlag, 127–44.

Laywine, Alison (2003). "Kant on Sensibility and Understanding in the 1770s." *Canadian Journal of Philosophy* 33: 443–82.

Lehmann, Gerhard (1969). *Beiträge zur Geschichte und Interpretation des Philosophie Kants.* Berlin: de Gruyter.

Louden, Robert B. (2000). *Kant's Impure Ethics: From Rational Beings to Human Beings.* Oxford: Oxford University Press.

Marcucci, Silvio (2001). "Système scientifique et système philosophique. Kant et Linné" in Ingeborg Schüssler ed., *Kant, les années 1796–1803. Opus postumum.* Paris: Vrin, 107–26.

Mathieu, Vittorio (1989). *Kants Opus postumum.* Ed. Gerd Held. Frankfurt: Klostermann.

McNulty, Bennett (2015). "Rehabilitating the Regulative Use of Reason: Kant on Empirical and Chemical Laws." *Studies in History and Philosophy of Science* 54: 1–10.

Messina, James (2017). "Kant's Necessitation Account of Laws and the Nature of Natures" in Michela Massimi and Angela Breitenbach eds., *Kant and the Laws of Nature*. Cambridge: Cambridge University Press, 131–49.

Pollok, Konstantin (2017). *Kant's Theory of Normativity: Exploring the Space of Reason*. Cambridge: Cambridge University Press.

Reichenbach, Hans [1920] (1965). *The Theory of Relativity and A Priori Knowledge*. Trans. Maria Reichenbach. Berkeley: University of California Press.

Rollman, Veit Justus (2015). *Apperzeption und dynamisches Naturgesetzt in Kants Opus Postumum*. Berlin: de Gruyter.

Schick, Stefan (2006). *Vermittelte Unmittelbarkeit. Jacobis "Salto mortale" als Konzept zur Aufhebung des Gegensatzes von Glaube und Spekulation in der intellektuellen Anschauung der Vernunft*. Würzburg: Königshausen & Neumann.

Schlick, Moritz [1915] (2019). "Die philosophische Bedeutung des Relativitätsprinzips" in Fynn Ole Engler ed., *Texte zu Einsteins Relativitätstheorie*. Hamburg: Meiner, 3–56.

Schwaiger, Clemens (2004). "Denken des 'Übersinnlichen' bei Kant. Zu Herkunft und Verwendung einer Schlüsselkategorie seiner praktischen Metaphysik" in Norbert Fischer ed., *Kants Metaphysik und Religionsphilosophie*. Hamburg: Meiner, 331–45.

Stang, Nicolas F. (2013). "Adickes on Double Affection" in Stefano Bacin, Alfredo Ferrarin, Claudio La Rocca, and Margit Ruffing eds., *Kant und die Philosophie in weltbürgerlicher Absicht. Akten des XI. Kant-Kongresses 2010*. Berlin: de Gruyter, 787–98.

  (2015). "Who's Afraid of Double Affection?" *Philosophers' Imprint* 15.18: 1–28.

Stark, Werner (1993). *Nachforschungen zu Briefen und Handschriften Immanuel Kants*. Berlin: Akademie Verlag.

Sturm, Thomas (2009). *Kant und die Wissenschaften vom Menschen*. Paderborn: Mentis.

Thorndike, Oliver (2018). *Kant's Transition Project and Late Philosophy: Connecting the Opus postumum and Metaphysics of Morals*. London: Bloomsbury.

Tuschling, Burkhard (1971). *Metaphysische und transzendentale Dynamik in Kants opus postumum*. Berlin: de Gruyter.

Vaihinger, Hans (1891). "Rezension zu Albrecht Krause, *Das nachgelassene Werk Immanuel Kants.*" *Archiv für Geschichte der Philosophie* 4: 731–6.

(1911). *Die Philosophie des Als-Ob. System der theoretischen, praktischen und religiösen Fiktionen der Menschheit auf Grund eines idealistischen Positivismus.* Berlin: Reuther & Reichard.

Watkins, Eric (2019). *Kant on Laws.* Cambridge: Cambridge University Press.

Westphal, Kenneth R. (1995). "Kant's Dynamic Constructions." *Journal of Philosophical Research* 20: 382–429.

Willaschek, Marcus (2017). "Freedom as a Postulate" in Eric Watkins ed., *Kant on Persons and Agency.* Cambridge: Cambridge University Press.

(2018). *Kant on the Sources of Metaphysics: The Dialectic of Pure Reason.* Cambridge: Cambridge University Press.

Zöller, Günter (2001). "'Die Seele des Systems': Systembegriff und Begriffssystem in Kants Transzendentalphilosophie" in Hans Friedrich Fulda und Jurgen Stolzenberg eds., *Architektonik und System in der Philosophie Kants. System der Vernunft.* Hamburg: Meiner, 53–72.

Acknowledgements

For their valuable comments on earlier drafts of this Element, I thank Franziska Aigner, Hammam Aldouri, Giampiero Basile, Jeffrey Edwards, Daniela Helbig, Jacqueline Karl, Luciano Perulli, Clinton Tolley, Eric Watkins, the audience of the 2021 Leuven Kant conference, and the participants of a History of Philosophy Roundtable at University of California, San Diego. Particular thanks to Des Hogan, for many insightful suggestions, and to Karin de Boer, both for her comments on the manuscript and for her intellectual generosity in general. The research for this Element was supported by the Research Foundation – Flanders (FWO).

Cambridge Elements $\equiv$

The Philosophy of Immanuel Kant

Desmond Hogan
Princeton University
Desmond Hogan joined the philosophy department at Princeton in 2004. His interests include Kant, Leibniz and German rationalism, early modern philosophy, and questions about causation and freedom. Recent work includes 'Kant on the Foreknowledge of Contingent Truths', *Res Philosophica* 91 (1) (2014); 'Kant's Theory of Divine and Secondary Causation', in Brandon Look (ed.) *Leibniz and Kant*, Oxford University Press (2021); 'Kant and the Character of Mathematical Inference', in Carl Posy and Ofra Rechter (eds.) *Kant's Philosophy of Mathematics Vol. I*, Cambridge University Press (2020).

Howard Williams
University of Cardiff
Howard Williams was appointed Honorary Distinguished Professor at the Department of Politics and International Relations, University of Cardiff in 2014. He is also Emeritus Professor in Political Theory at the Department of International Politics, Aberystwyth University, a member of the Coleg Cymraeg Cenedlaethol (Welsh-language national college) and a Fellow of the Learned Society of Wales. He is the author of *Marx* (1980); *Kant's Political Philosophy* (1983); *Concepts of Ideology* (1988); *Hegel, Heraclitus and Marx's Dialectic* (1989); *International Relations in Political Theory* (1992); *International Relations and the Limits of Political Theory* (1996); *Kant's Critique of Hobbes: Sovereignty and Cosmopolitanism* (2003); *Kant and the End of War* (2012) and is currently editor of the journal *Kantian Review*. He is writing a book on the Kantian legacy in political philosophy for a new series edited by Paul Guyer.

Allen Wood
Indiana University
Allen Wood is Ward W. and Priscilla B. Woods Professor Emeritus at Stanford University. He was a John S. Guggenheim Fellow at the Free University in Berlin, a National Endowment for the Humanities Fellow at the University of Bonn and Isaiah Berlin Visiting Professor at the University of Oxford. He is on the editorial board of eight philosophy journals, five book series and *The Stanford Encyclopedia of Philosophy*. Along with Paul Guyer, Professor Wood is co-editor of The Cambridge Edition of the Works of Immanuel Kant and translator of the *Critique of Pure Reason*. He is the author or editor of a number of other works, mainly on Kant, Hegel and Karl Marx. His most recently published books are *Fichte's Ethical Thought*, Oxford University Press (2016) and *Kant and Religion*, Cambridge University Press (2020). Wood is a member of the American Academy of Arts and Sciences.

About the Series

This Cambridge Elements series provides an extensive overview of Kant's philosophy and its impact upon philosophy and philosophers. Distinguished Kant specialists provide an up-to-date summary of the results of current research in their fields and give their own take on what they believe are the most significant debates influencing research, drawing original conclusions.

Cambridge Elements ⁼

The Philosophy of Immanuel Kant

Elements in the Series

Kant on the Rationality of Morality
Paul Guyer

The Guarantee of Perpetual Peace
Wolfgang Ertl

Kant and Global Distributive Justice
Sylvie Loriaux

Anthropology from a Kantian Point of View
Robert B. Louden

Introducing Kant's Critique of Pure Reason
Paul Guyer and Allen Wood

Kant's Theory of Conscience
Samuel Kahn

*Rationalizing (*Vernünfteln)
Martin Sticker

Kant and the French Revolution
Reidar Maliks

The Kantian Federation
Luigi Caranti

The Politics of Beauty: A Study of Kant's Critique of Taste
Susan Meld Shell

Kant's Theory of Labour
Jordan Pascoe

Kant's Late Philosophy of Nature: The Opus postumum
Stephen Howard

A full series listing is available at: www.cambridge.org/EPIK

Printed in the United States
by Baker & Taylor Publisher Services